29

P.T. BRENT

P T Brent

First Printing 17 March 2013

Copyright © 2012 by P.T. Brent

ISBN: 978-1482395563

Library of Congress Control Number: 2013903518

PUBLISHER'S NOTE

Printed in the United States

Dedication

29 is dedicated to Laura Aroon* my extraordinary daughter who makes the sun rise for her father each and every day

and to:

Thomas Edward Prentice USMC/TSOCP** my calabash*** son/ nephew and my favorite Marine.

*Gaelic for darling

**another mystery

***In Hawaiian, calabash is an adopted relative, not necessarily of the same bloodline.

Accolades

There are so many extraordinary people who have made this work possible. They know who they are and that they are not only appreciated but, indeed, treasured.

Mahalo Nui Loa & aloha from the fairest islands ever nestled on planet earth.

P.T. Brent

People may not always like me . . .
but they will remember me.

Colonel John Richard Bates's favorite quote by

P.T. Brent, 10 November 1988

A Foreword

by Colonel John Richard Bates,
United States Marine Corps (retired)[1]

U.S. Marines by their very culture are strong, bold, disciplined . . . and ultimately victorious.

The Irish know how to make something from nothing . . . and still find cheeky humor in a "hard knock" life.

Catholics care deeply about their God, their country and their fellow man.

Marine Irish-Catholic P.T. Brent has lived an extraordinary life and his "finish line" is still beyond the horizon. A product of his environment and experiences, he tells of an austere childhood as a young man growing up in a one-room apartment with his grandmother, lighted by the glow of a single bulb hanging from a bare wire. From those exceptionally humble beginnings, he has mastered the art of understanding what makes people "tick." And in sales, he has learned what makes them "buy."

Unlike most of us, he knows how to disarm hostility with a smile and unexpected kindness thereby humbling, turning the tables on and often embarrassing his adversary. Mr. Brent, on determination

---

[1] Author's Note: Colonel John Richard Bates is one helluva of a fighting Leatherneck. He was in three wars for his country, suffered enough to earn three Purple Hearts, and served 33 years in the most sharply disciplined and aggressive fighting force the world has ever known.

and personality, has gone from "nothing" to being featured in the book *Above and Beyond* (Rudy Socha, Turner Publishing), a "who's who" listing of some of the most influential Marines in the corporate world following their service to their country.

When Patrick's name surfaces in conversation, more often than not, the word "outrageous" is spoken by many—and often. Usually, the term is uttered with a smile as people relate either personal or relayed stories of his shenanigans, elaborate practical jokes or verbal jousting with business competitors. This book is a short, personal and humble overview of success through determination. Let it not be lost on the reader that there is another P.T.B. to whom Patrick Timothy Brent might find blood ties. His last name would be *Barnum* of three-ring circus fame.

Coincidence? You decide.

Colonel John Richard Bates, United States Marine Corps (retired)
Running buddy, world travel buddy and practical joke assistant to P.T.B. for over three decades

A Perspective on the Author

by Glenn W. Schmidt[2]

P.T. Brent is a relatively new author but an old hand at making things happen.

He has an inquiring mind, along with a mental and physical toughness—and he lives with a standard of integrity that sets a high benchmark for his colleagues in life.

He is a devoted father and a patriot with unbridled pride in his country and the United States Marine Corps.

I was the guy who worked with Patrick Brent after he conquered National Cash Register (NCR)—and before he acquired the first of several companies. At University Computing Company, we climbed the management ladder together, with many episodes of anguish and joy, as well as a few business conquests along the way.

The pages that follow will allow us as readers to share some of his life stories. As a few of these memoirs unfolded, I was an admiring spectator. Others are more recent—but delightful surprises. Hard work took P.T. from the inner city of Chicago to San Francisco, then to Hawaii and around the world—and he's never forgotten those humble beginnings. Throughout the drama that is the life of the

---

[2] Author's Note: Mr. Glenn Schmidt is the most extraordinary motivator of men and gifted business executive this author has ever met. He is also an exceptional father and husband—ask P.T. Schmidt, his son.

author, you will find audacity, humor and drive.

Get ready for some fun . . . as well as some serious moments that involve leaders of the military and heroes of our country.

Glenn W. Schmidt
Retired businessman
Aiken, South Carolina

Sea Stories

VOLUME III - IRISHMAN

VOLUME IV - CORRESPONDENT

VOLUME V - LEATHERNECK

EPILOGUE

AFTERMATH

There are seven hallmarks hidden in the W.G.C. (World's Greatest City) Skyline on the front cover. Can you identify them all?

Volume I

ENTREPRENEUR

Nothing in the world can take the place of persistence. Talent will not; nothing is more common than unsuccessful men with talent. Genius will not; unrewarded genius is almost a proverb. Education will not; the world is full of educated derelicts. Persistence and determination alone are omnipotent.

Calvin Coolidge

Chapter 1 is dedicated to Marine Sergeant Gerard Butzen of Platoon 282 Parris Island, who set the bar, along with our DIs—one helluva Jarhead.

1
Fortuna Fortes Juvat

Motto of the Island Warriors aka the 2ⁿᵈ Battalion 3ʳᵈ Marines in Kaneohe: ("Fortune Favors the Brave")[3]

After a thorough study of human nature, it can be concluded that brave people—those who exhibit boldness—even though they sometimes err in judgment, usually are more successful than the people who simply stand back in the shadows and watch life. Such is the case in business, combat and romance. These three arenas of life provide an infinite variety of such situations—miniature life lessons simply waiting to be observed and absorbed. The times when determination has been at its peak for me came after long periods of drought. My life, bereft of romance and concurrent with sky-high testosterone . . .

Dateline: Adult ice-skating review in the Boulevard Room of the Conrad Hilton Hotel,[4] WGC.[5]

The occasion was a black tie affair after Mayor Daly's St. Patrick's Day Party. Charlotte Farr, a member of one of the more affluent Irish-Catholic families in Chicago-land, was my date for the evening and

---

[3] Ray Kroc, founder of McDonald's, also has this homily on the wall in the office of every manager in his company.
[4] at the time, the world's largest hotel
[5] WGC – World's Greatest City

later almost made me a married man. Up against her stunning green gown, my tuxedo looked exactly what it was—a fifteen-dollar, second-hand affair.

Seven beautiful female ice-skaters and seven, (what turned out to be) mostly gay, male ice-skaters composed the ice-skating troupe. Together, they performed a fun, albeit racy, adult show, and one of them made my heart race a little faster. Carol Loren, a skater with long dark hair, had three years of experience with the Ice Capades in Europe and in America—and she possessed a cosmopolitan flair, a certain sophistication, that flowed through every movement. She stared at me throughout the evening. Later, it would be revealed that it was kind of a thing she did. During a show, Carol would pick someone out of the crowd and direct all of her attention his way, honing in—as if she were performing a private show for a captivated audience of one. On this St. Patrick's Day, she selected me; our position in the audience probably helped: we sat right next to the rail of the ice rink, having cocktails in nightclub fashion.

Carol kept this up through the entire show. Toward the end, when the cast released balloons to the audience, she skated up to the sideboards, leaned over, and gave me a green balloon. With this gesture, Charlotte finally took notice; my only reply was, "Well . . . guess she's Irish." Later, when Charlotte was busy, I went backstage, bluffing to the maître d' that Carol was a former schoolmate of mine. It's unlikely he believed that, but it was good enough to grant me access. A few minutes later, Carol Loren tapped me on the shoulder.

We dated for a couple of months, but the nightclub setting of our relationship wore me out and almost ruined my career. She introduced me to a different way of life, one that was not particularly healthy for my long-term prosperity. Eventually, she dropped me for a famous race jockey and life went on. Our relationship was more of a sprint, but this average-looking guy of less than considerable means was happy to have run with one of the most fascinating women in the western world.

Later in life, during a performance of the "George M." musical in San Francisco, a woman mesmerized me from the stage. She was the kind of woman who sets off a "magnitude seven" earthquake when she walks into a room. Her long auburn hair lit the fire, and those nightingale pipes kept it smoldering. Her name was Patricia O'Connell. After calling her from my office, identifying myself as Chairman/CEO of a rather prestigious company, and arranging a tour for her, we embarked upon a short, but grand romance. As a famous lady from literature (Anne of Green Gables) once said, "People who haven't red hair don't know what trouble is." Patricia also came close to wearing me out, and she too banished this gentleman—but not because of my brazen gestures. One can get away with audacious behavior—as long as it's backed by sincerity and respect.

Yet later, the CBS morning show ran a segment about a little seaside town in Alaska where most of the residents put on wetsuits and surfed on an almost daily basis; a rather remarkable young lady in the Alaskan television crowd caught my attention. Socializing with her required the assistance of a few CBS employees. It was another brief flirtation—all in good fun.

Whether in business, romance, or any other endeavor in life, it is a good idea to think twice and to be careful, but not to the extent that one is never bold enough to go out there and face repeated rejections. It is my belief that for every successful salesman, this principle holds true. They are devoted to a disciplined pursuit of their goals. Clearly, that is all that many of the stars in the world are: good salesmen. All good and successful salesmen have had multiple rejections! Our current president[6] and President Richard Nixon lost major elections in a wipeout but stayed out there and kept trying and trying again.

People ask me where I learned determination. It was at a place called Parris Island, South Carolina. I learned it from each and every Marine officer and NCO I met. I learned leadership and determination 24 hours a day, seven days a week from each and every Marine. Why? Because our Corps is immersed in a culture of excellence founded on virtue and discipline. Of my many titles—chairman, CEO, United States Polo Association governor, etc.—a standout has always been U.S. Marine. The pride that comes with being a Marine is like nothing else. With determination, even a fair salesman can suffer rejection after rejection and charge ahead to get the mission done. Some of the

---

[6] Barack Obama

world's finest scholars are merely good salesmen too. One exception may be scientists, but even scientists are always charging ahead and trying new ground. Eventually, the fear of rejection or failure is supplanted by resilience and—yes, victory. Winston Churchill advised us never to yield to force or to "the apparently overwhelming might of the enemy." In a famous speech at the Harrow School, he said, "Never give in—never, never, never, never, in nothing great or small, large or petty, never give in except to convictions of honor and good sense."

Be brave, and eventually, you'll be able to embrace that last part.

*A young man who does not have what
it takes to perform military service
is not likely to have what it takes
to make a living.*

John F. Kennedy

Chapter 2-alfa is dedicated toMarc Hamilton Paiva, former president of Hamilton Taft, whose ineluctable energy and integrity offered leadership second to none.

2-alfa
Ice Cream Tricycles to Pearl Harbor

Apparently, it is possible to be an entrepreneur for almost a generation prior to ever learning the word *entrepreneur*. A French word for *businessman*, this term comes with the underlying notion that business is full of risks and therefore calls for initiative. What makes someone an entrepreneur? In my opinion, entrepreneurs probably are born more out of necessity than from true desire, or at least that's true for me.

Never having a family to mentor me or people willing to hire me or help me during my formative years, my early decisions were easy to understand. My desire was to do my own thing. At the age of 13, this enterprising lad was counted among the newspaper boys of Northlake, Illinois. In addition, Mrs. Werneke employed me during the summer months. Mrs. Werneke owned three ice cream carts that were basically tricycles with big boxes in their centers. These boxes held popsicles, ice cream bars and many other confections tucked beneath a couple of slabs of dry ice. Luckily, Mrs. Werneke took to me and gave me the middle route which was near my home, enabling me to make an extra four, five or six dollars a day based on the one and two-penny commissions earned by selling eight to ten-cent popsicles and ice cream bars.

After employing me for two consecutive summers, Mrs. Werneke told me that she was going to retire. How could a lad convince Mrs. Werneke that the "R" word was not a wise course of action? Instead, I went to my mother and stepfather (who had adopted me by then) and convinced them to buy Mrs. Werneke's three ice cream carts. My plan was to set up the ice cream carts along the side of the garage and do all of the work, but the profits would be theirs. This is how, at the tender age of 15, I went out on the market and started finding extra carts that could be repaired. My skill as a bicycle repairman became prodigious. Our original fleet of ice cream carts grew to six! Later, we opened a branch in Maywood with six more carts and some Cushman motor scooters that had larger ice cream capacities. We operated both branches for two summers. It was quite a kick, at age 16, to have my own command, albeit, under my parents' auspices. My mother and father operated the business by themselves and eventually sold it after my college education was complete. There

is still a Marine general named Melvin who owes me 10 cents for a Fudgesicle.

After working for two very large companies, NCR[7] and UCC,[8] my wanderlust and desire to live in San Francisco took hold. Finding a job in San Francisco that was equal to my jobs in the Midwest was daunting. It seemed that the top guys from Harvard, Yale and the other Ivy League schools went to California for work, so the job market was extremely competitive. Staying in San Francisco would require some ingenuity and collaboration with some acquaintances from New Orleans who wanted to start an airline ticketing business. That's how my first "grown up" entrepreneurial endeavor, Western 29, was launched. To this day, the reason for its name is a long-held secret—only my daughter and two or three other people know. Most people would find it hard to believe that Western 29 was started with $1,200 and one extra phone in the guest room of my apartment (actually in my buddy Nick Calvert's room) at 944 Corbett Avenue, at the top of Twin Peaks, in San Francisco.

Originally, Western 29 was a licensee of the airline ticketing business in New Orleans, but when that company suffered a series of embezzlements and other similar disasters, the owners offered to sell it to me. At that time, the company was virtually worthless, but after cutting the owners a deal for $20,000 (most of it in a note), ownership reverted to me. Jim Nappo, my executive vice president

[7] National Cash Register
[8] University Computing Company

27

and partner at the time, helped me persuade General Electric and other good people to underwrite Western 29 and help us. We believed that the airlines eventually would do away with manual ticketing, and our mission was to replace the manual system with a computerized system that would handle airline reservations, ticketing, itineraries, invoices, accounting and bank reports for the entire travel industry. It was a rough go! Imagine all digital and paperless.

We did really well with marketing and sales. Our first clients were American Express, Greyhound and several other large travel companies of the time, including Tradewind Tours[9] in Honolulu, Hawaii. Friendships with Bob McGregor and Fred Dailey in Hawaii, 30 years of playing polo,[10] and falling in love with horses, resulted from the business partnership between Western 29 and Tradewind Tours.

Two distinct moments come to mind when I sat on my bed, in my home at the corner of 29th and Lincoln, across from the Golden Gate Park in San Francisco, and considered wrapping it up and closing down the business. Fortunately, on both occasions, the following day was sunny, and my morale went up; both times, we charged ahead. Eventually, we sold the company to McDonald-Douglas. When we sold, our sales totaled $28 million, and the software is still owned by United/Continental Airlines in Texas. Some of the Western

---

[9] the world's largest wholesale travel company
[10] the world's greatest sport!

29 forms and techniques are considered legendary in the travel industry.

After the sale of Western 29, ABC Television employed me for a short period of time. However, the first couple of post-merger years were very uncomfortable for me, partially because the helm was not mine, and neither was capacity for taking orders from other managers.

Later on, a new initiative was Hamilton Taft & Company, the first company to do payroll tax reporting for large corporations. After a company's payroll was done, Hamilton Taft maximized the float for federal, state and local taxes. The float benefit was returned to both the tax-paying corporation and Hamilton Taft through the collection of fees and float interest income. Hamilton Taft contracted with some of the largest corporations in the country and grew to over $5 billion a year in assets flowing through our operation. Although we received acquisition offers from the First National Bank of Chicago, Bank of America and the Cigna Insurance Company in Connecticut, we chose Cigna because we thought they would take better care of the people. On the day of the merger, this entrepreneur wisely decided to leave the company.

Post Hamilton Taft, there was a series of "starts"; some businesses were successful and others were not. There was also a stint as president of CRS, a subsidiary of Charles Schwab. Eventually, all of my endeavors lead to the genesis of Bradford Adams & Company, a publishing firm and the very company that set me up to do combat journalism. After Bradford Adams came my stint with Windjammer Cruises. Then my partner, Jim Sharp, and I started Sharp 29, and that was followed by my investment in two small hotel properties in Hawaii. All of these businesses were preceded by the creation and management of the Pearl Harbor Visitor Center.

The Pearl Harbor Visitor Center was created on an expeditionary basis, with the intention of establishing a permanent center with a $35 million loan from Central Pacific Bank. We had a 65-year lease, so a permanent center seemed feasible. However, local politics, coupled with a lack of support and cooperation from our non-profit neighbors, doomed the venture, as is well documented by Jerry Coffee, in his kind article in "Travel Weekly."

After three years, we closed the Pearl Harbor Visitor Center with style and form, and we were successful in placing all 150 crew members in jobs elsewhere. Once again, the ever-resourceful Irishman moved on to other pursuits. The net profit from the operation was $17,000, pending resolution of a small six-figure fee from the Hunt Building Company.

Becoming an entrepreneur is so much more than writing and filing paperwork and being responsible enough to oversee all of the legal and administrative matters involved in starting up a business. As evidence of that, the vast majority of companies—a staggering 90 percent or more—that are incorporated in a given year are not paying their corporate taxes four or five years later. Why? Simply put—

because most people start businesses for the wrong reasons. Many spouses of my friends have gone into the clothing business or travel business or the food business because they eat, travel and wear clothes. These are **WRONG** reasons for starting businesses. People who start business should be business-minded, first and foremost; even more than that, they should be sales people!

Forget all the red tape and bureaucracy. Start your company. Produce your product. Go out and sell something as fast as possible and have "sales" leading the charge. Production, accounting and paperwork can always be done. Once you have dramatic sales and significant revenue coming in, time and history will repair all difficulties. Time and time again, people establish bureaucracies filled with lawyers, accountants and red tape—and never sell anything. Of course, they go to the stock market and they go to good people to raise investment capital. Sometimes, they even have public issues of stock, but they have lost sight of the business mission. The mission is to go out, sell, and get a product in front of potential clients who will constitute a revenue base that will someday lead to long-term success. These principles of how to start up new business ventures should be taught in universities and business schools, but they are not. Instead, universities and business schools first teach people all about the red tape—the bureaucracy stuff—and potential entrepreneurs lose sight of the mission.

Perhaps there was a lack of intelligence or start-up money, or perhaps, I was just a born salesman and realized early on that the best thing to do was to go out and sell my product first. That's been the story of all my ventures. Hopefully, future generations won't lose sight of the mission—as it is this style of business that keeps both the economy and the heart of the true entrepreneur pumping.

United States Senate

SUITE 722, HART SENATE OFFICE BUILDING
WASHINGTON, DC 20510-1102
(202) 224-3934

February 23, 2007

Mr. Patrick Brent
Honolulu, Hawaii 96814

Dear Mr. Brent:

I am writing to thank you for your service to the tens of thousands of visitors to the USS Arizona and other historic attractions through your establishment and operation of the Pearl Harbor Visitor Center.

I must confess to you that when the big white tent first went up, I was disturbed that it was a blight upon the majestic and somber view plane that looks out from Halawa Landing. To your credit, you acknowledged the concerns and adjusted accordingly, including sharing the economic opportunities with some of the historic partners, and in particular the Bowfin. Your employees were knowledgeable about the history of the area, which they enthusiastically shared with many a visitor. There is no questions that your operation, the Pearl Harbor Visitor Center, brought to light the lack of basic amenities that were being offered to our visitors, who were faced with a wait for hour upon hour, oftentimes without shelter, a meal or activities to help pass the time.

I would venture to say that you bruised the conscience of the National Park Service and Navy, and you woke up the historic partners – Arizona, Missouri, Bowfin, Aviation Museum – about the need to provide a better level of accomodations for the visitor. You seized upon some economic opportunities while stepping into some emotional territory.

In the end, the Navy made the decision to amicably buy out the Hunt Development contract to operate at the Halawa Landing, and in turn hand it over to the National Park Service. A year's notice was provided to all vendors. While an inquiry was made regarding the possibility of continuing on a month to month basis until suitable alternative visitor accommodations were established, the Park Services responded to the Navy that together with historic partners, they were confident that the visitors would be taken care of. I have deferred to their judgement, but I have asked Admiral Alexander of Navy Region Hawaii that he continue to monitor the situation, with an eye first and foremost on the welfare of the visitor.

I know you hoped that it would have ended differently, however, I hope you will find solace in knowing that your actions will result in a better overall visitor experience in and about the memorials of Pearl Harbor.

Aloha,

DANIEL K. INOUYE
United States Senator

Ode to the Number 29

1. Twenty-nine (29) is the natural number following 28 and preceding 30. Seriously, check it out, Glenn.

2. The lunar month is 29 days. Check it out, P nmi H

3. Saturn requires over 29 years to orbit the sun.

4. Twenty-nine: the number of days in February during leap years. Women are permitted to propose to men—look out!

5. What country is located 29 North latitude and 29 East longitude? Hey Ritchie, it is Egypt.

6. In 1929—there was the start of the Wall Street Crash at the New York Stock Exchange. "Black Tuesday" was the following week on October 29, 1929.

7. The atomic bomb which won WWII for the Army Air Corps in the Pacific (Boeing, USA) was dropped on Hiroshima by the Enola Gay, a B-29 aircraft commanded by Colonel Paul Tibbetts.

8. South Africa held its first interracial national election on 29 April; Nelson Mandela was elected.

9. The Marines' Hymn was arranged for band concerts by Edward Van Loock in 1929.

10. "Iwakalua Eiwa" is the Hawaiian translation for 29; Mahalo, Paula.

11. Twentynine Palms is the name of the Marine Corps Air Ground Combat Center affectionately referred to by Marines as "Twentynine Stumps."

12. The name of the town Twentynine Palms, California, is the Marine base where this author once trained for desert warfare.

13. Frank Sinatra, the Andrews Sisters, and Doris Day sang about "The Lady from 29 Palms" who left 29 broken hearts in 29 different parts.

14. Officials with the penitentiary Alcatraz claimed no prisoner had successfully escaped during 29 years of federal operation. A total of 36 prisoners made 14 escape attempts, two men trying twice; 23 were caught, six were shot and killed during their escape, two drowned, and five are listed as "missing and presumed drowned." Reality: they swam to the infamous Dolphin Club circa Fisherman's Wharf in San Francisco and had a few cool ones with Buck Swannack, Chuck Vogt, Don Reid and Walt Stack and failed to have a press conference. The Feds lied.

15. In the Glenn Miller song, the "Chattanooga Choo Choo" departs track 29, Grand Central Station, New York City.

16. Twenty-nine is the number of letters in the Turkish, Finnish, Swedish, Faroese, Danish and Norwegian alphabets.

17. Notre Dame broke Army's record for most consecutive wins in college football by defeating Navy, 40-0 in Baltimore on 29 October 1949.

18. Twenty-nine: the number of Knuts in one Sickle in the fictional currency in the Harry Potter novels.

19. Interstate 29 is a U.S. freeway that runs from Missouri to North Dakota.

20. Twenty-nine is the highest possible score in a hand of Cribbage or Khanhoo.

21. Twenty-nine is the number of the French department of Finistère. Ask Terrence Yorga, a 29 comm. expert.

22. On 29 July 1891, Laura Mabel Todd was born in Mount Pleasant, Iowa. Laura was the inspiration for the famous Laura Todd Cookies Bakeries—USA, Europe, Chicago, London, San Francisco and Paris.

23. All zip codes in the state of South Carolina, where Laura Todd's grandson once vacationed at Parris Island, begin with the digits *two and nine*. South Carolina is also the home of an infamous editor.

24. Irish history was made on the corner of 29th Avenue and Lincoln Way in San Francisco.

25. Western 29, Inc., based in San Francisco, was the first computer corporation to create and implement airline ticketing vis-a-vis nine major airlines, right Jim Nappo?

26. The 29th Olympiad was the 2008 Summer Olympics. During the 2012 Olympics, "God Save the Queen" was sung 29 times. Semper Fidelis, Sam.

27. A 29er is a mountain bike with 29-inch wheels.

28. It's often stated that 29 is the permanent age of Ramona Robertson and perhaps this author's I.Q.

29. TWENTY-NINE can be written out with exactly 29 toothpicks. Try it, Thomas (the doubting type).

    Many claim the real secret of 2929 is in order ... the age of the editor, Amanda, and the author, P.T.'s I.Q.

*I've found that prayers work best
when you've got big players.*

Knute Rockne

Notre Dame

2-bravo
Adventures in Business

When my career as a salesman began, it seemed to me that everybody followed certain rules of salesmanship—take the price book and regulations and share them with customers, clients and friends. *But why?* To my way of thinking, most people did this, and still do this, because people are apprehensive about using their imaginations or adapting the rules to fit the old concept, "please the customer." At NCR, the company that gave me my first adult job, I rapidly learned that to compete with IBM, we had to offer our customers something imaginative in the form of services—something that our customers would never receive from a stodgy, by-the-numbers company like IBM.[11]

Here is my case in point—Fire Protection Industry in Chicago, the largest fire protection company in the Midwest. Fire Protection Industry's president wanted to move the company processes to a small computer or a large accounting machine, so he called in five of the seven major computer services—NCR, IBM, Burroughs, Univac and Control Data. The president was a big, overweight guy whose tie and pants were too short and moustache was too long, but his

---

[11] IBM stands for International Business Machines.

company was making a tremendous amount of money selling fire protection equipment. Everything in his office, including his toys and knickknacks, was fire-engine red.

Salesmen are born with an instinct and an ability to chat up receptionists. My goal was always to study every little detail in the outer lobby and to learn as much possible. On the day of my visit to Fire Protection Industry, the receptionist informed me that the president had met with IBM just prior to my morning appointment. Immediately, I loosened my tie, unbuttoned my shirt at the neck, took off my suit coat, and strolled into the president's office. While he chatted about his experiences with other vendors and what he wanted product-wise, my job was to appraise his office and its contents. Finally, the president looked at me and asked, "You know IBM machines come in blue, and they tell me yours come in tan. Is that true?" We both knew that he wanted something else, and my response gave him what he wanted.

"Sir, our machines come in fire-engine red. Every panel on every piece of equipment here will be fire-engine red." Twenty-four hours later, our contract was signed; and in a few weeks, NCR's tan computer panels were personally delivered, by me, to an auto paint shop to be painted . . . YES . . . fire-engine red.

A few months later, my work with NCR took me to the Angel Guardian Orphanage (A.G.O.). This orphanage was quite familiar to me; it had been my home as an adolescent. Both IBM and NCR had made multiple attempts to sell computers to the orphanage. NCR's file on Angel Guardian Orphanage was four or five inches thick, even though nothing had ever been sold to the orphanage. IBM had the same record with the orphanage as NCR. My visits to Angel Guardian Orphanage were not purely professional; the nuns and priests remembered me from my stay there eight or nine years earlier. They informed me that they had no money and no interest in computers, but they allowed me to put in a machine on a trial basis—if it were fully programmed and came with lessons from me. So, a machine was programmed for payroll, orphans' billing (the orphanage billed Cook County for expenses relating to some of the orphans), and a few other applications; then the little boy who grew up at Angel Guardian taught the nuns how to use the computer. Talk about role-reversal!

After the NCR machine had been at the orphanage for a few weeks, one of the nuns let me know that the IBM salesmen were back again and talking with members of the board who were mightily impressed with them and the name IBM. It appeared that my work might be for naught and that NCR might, indeed, be in trouble from a professional point of view. It was time to get out of there and gather my thoughts.

Just across Devon Avenue, the main street by the orphanage, was an old drugstore with an old-fashioned counter where patrons could get handmade milkshakes, grilled hamburgers, and other soda fountain favorites. The stool at the end of the counter provided a welcome respite, and a hamburger and cherry Coke fueled my thinking.

Upon my return to the orphanage, Sister Mary Therese said to me, "Patrick, Sister Dolores and I are very upset with you." My conscience was clear, so my response was, "Why?" And she replied, "I think you know why." The sisters' distress persisted all afternoon and into the next morning, until they wore me down to the point of confronting them. "You've got to tell me why [you're upset with me]." Sister Dolores and Sister Mary Therese jogged my memory with these words, the same rhetorical phrase they had used the day before: "We think you know why. Every A.G.O. young man knows from the beginning that the children here are not allowed to go across Devon Avenue and go into commercial businesses. Yesterday, you went on your own. We think you even had lunch there, and we don't like it at all." My 24 years and my job did not deter the sisters at all; to them, Patrick was still part of the A.G.O. family. That is how a 24-year-old businessman came to apologize to nuns for eating lunch at a drug-store.

Despite my transgression, the sisters did tell me to talk with Monsignor Diebold, since he and the board had been talking with IBM.

A.G.O.'s continued dialogue with IBM disconcerted me. Without stopping for the monsignor's secretary to announce me, I walked into his office and asked, "Monsignor, I just need to know . . . are you going to buy from IBM or the boy who used to live at Cottage 32?" He smiled and enjoyed the moment. Then he replied, "Patrick, we've long since planned to buy NCR. Somebody just wanted to give IBM a chance to say *hello*. We're buying your machine next week." Yet again, a little boldness on my part sealed the deal. Sometimes the work we do "on spec" is richly rewarded. In any case, it's all about finding a way to show a customer what you can do.

For several months prior to March 1972, in New Orleans and Houston, my work consisted of preparing a new company, originally called COMTRAV and later renamed Western 29, that would be the first to offer automated reservations and ticketing for travel agents—the first in the world. My original plan was to go out to the West Coast and work as a licensing agent, but the company, based in the Monte Leon Hotel in New Orleans,[12] was having problems, ranging from technical issues to embezzlement. After a few demonstrations of Western 29's product in San Francisco, the responses from interested companies were good, and that was promising.

At that time, the world's largest travel agency was the Haley Corporation. All of Haley's services and processes—tickets, itineraries, invoices and the subsequent accounting, bank reports,

---

[12] This was the birthplace of my first "grown-up" business.

receivables, general ledger, etc.—had to be done by entering and re-entering the data. The people at Haley found the demonstrations of our product revolutionary. Western 29 could provide them with the single-entry answer to their multiple-entry data problem.

It should be noted here that Western 29 was started in the guest room of my small, two-bedroom apartment on Twin Peaks in San Francisco with $1,200. Eventually, Western 29, would gross $28 million in revenues, but at the beginning, we had one customer, Montana Travel, in Bozeman, and a few other prospects. My contact with Haley had started at the top, with the executive board; they were apprehensive and wanted to send two executives to New Orleans to visit the Western 29 offices.

One of the age-old problems in sales and business is to have credibility with your first client or to have credibility when you have no experience, and yet deserve it because you have a worthwhile product or worthwhile business idea. In advance of the executives' flight to New Orleans, Jim Nappo and my other friends, who were still down there, arranged to have my old company offices quickly and completely redecorated with a new corporate logo. Everyone was briefed, the decorators went in, and our corporate identity was transformed ahead of Haley Corp's visit. After another demonstration of the product, Haley Corporation became one of our long-term, happy customers. This covert operation has the distinction of most closely resembling a *Mission Impossible* situation in my life. Perhaps this Irishman misled those Haley Corp. executives, but they had to see what we could do in a way that spoke to them. In the long run, hopefully, it was for the good of everyone.

The great events of the world
take place in the brain . . .

Oscar Wilde

Chapter 3-alfa is dedicated to Mary Ann Prentice, a cosmopolitan style lady, the best of NCR Chicago—one extraordinarily gifted programmer and a calabash member of P.T. Brent's family.
God bless her!

3-alfa
Reflection on Perception

My earlier years of employment were spent with National Cash Register (NCR) in Chicago, selling accounting machines to hotels and hospitals. My previous experience included working as an auditor at several prominent Chicago hotels during college, so approaching hotels as prospective clients felt natural to me as a salesman. During my second year with NCR, this determined salesman's figures ranked highest in the division, which encompassed the 12 north-central states.

With all of this success coming during my second year as an NCR employee, it was apparent it was time to become a "sailor." My mornings were spent on programs and various things, but Grant Park Harbor[13], located just down the street from the NCR building, beckoned. Many sailboats and a couple of yacht clubs were visible from NCR's windows.

One of the clubs, *Columbia*, catered mostly to sailors, and was inexpensive to join. Ken Weirmeyer, a grand guy, ran *Columbia*. In an effort to recruit young people, *Columbia* made the dues inexpensive for the under-30 crowd; and if you were under 25, *Columbia* almost

---

[13] Grant Park – the same place where Barack Obama accepted his win in the 2008 presidential election.

paid you to join. The decision to sign up for *Columbia's* sailing school originally came with the intention of concentrating on sailing mostly on weekends. However, sailing school required me to slip out of the office some afternoons to attend sessions. By May, Ken and I had hit it off, and when he took out three or four young ladies for a sailing lesson, he took me along as his assistant instructor. In addition to having a marvelous time on Lake Michigan, my sailing skills were becoming adroit.

While trying to do my best at my full-time job, sailing and enjoying Lake Michigan were creating a wrinkle in my workday. Each afternoon around 1300 or 1400 hours, one could find me at the yacht club, rigging a Rhoades 19 sailboat with Ken and heading out for a good time, usually returning around 1630. How does one offset one of the greatest summers ever with missed work? For me, it involved tweaking my daily agenda to create space and time for sailing.

My mornings that summer began around 0500, when all of my programming and paperwork was undertaken, followed by mid-morning sales calls. In addition to rising so early, lunch was skipped in favor of passing three or four hours on the water, then returning to the office by 1700 or 1800 hours to work a couple of hours before going home. It was possible to go from the yacht club back to work because of the shower facilities at the club. All summer, each and every day, this was the scenario of my life. Sailing proficiency and a stellar tan reflected time spent on Lake Michigan. The corporate culture at NCR was formal and traditional, meaning no amount of sales would be enough for the managers to advocate my nontraditional schedule.

Isn't it amazing—the perceptions that people have and the realties on which they're based?

Jerry Graham, our branch manager at NCR Chicago, was a "Taipan" who made an astronomical salary by managing 12 states and all divisions of NCR—cash registers, adding machines, computers and accounting machines. Although Mr. Graham had an office on the top floor, he was a gentleman who believed in the old adage: "management by walking around," and this wasn't something unknown to me.

It would seem that some workers toil dutifully and produce well, but they may fall short of the boss's "A List" if they're not found at their posts often enough. The opposite is surely true, but ultimately, one must invest in both work time and face time.

Mr. Graham held a monthly sales meeting for all 400 NCR salesmen in the Midwest region. In a giant auditorium, at 0700, military marches and John Philip Souza music roused the attendees, and Mr. Graham gave riveting, inspirational speeches to encourage his salesmen to bring in record numbers. Needless to say, Jerry Graham was quite the leader.

As this particular meeting took place, we were approaching the end of September; sailing season was rapidly winding down as fall and winter weather approached Chicago.[14] My NCR buddies and I went into the auditorium and listened as Mr. Graham gave a long speech on the personification of a great NCR man. He spoke of long hours and dedication to NCR's mission, and he said, "That's what we all should aspire to be." My summer sailing tan was still glowing as we sat there admiring the gentleman Jerry Graham was describing and not knowing who he could be.

Finally, to my shock and awe, Mr. Graham asked for Patrick Timothy Brent to come up on stage. One or two of my buddies knew of my summer activity, although they were not aware of the frequency of my sailing; they looked at me as I stood. For my part, my self-given bonus of a half-day of sailing every day might have caught up with me. Even so, I marched up to the stage and stood there at parade rest while Jerry Graham talked about *THE* NCR man. He said, "As you know, I like to go through the building when I first get here in the early morning, which is usually before sunrise, and again before I leave for the afternoon, which is always after sundown. And every time I stop

---

[14] World's Greatest City

on the third floor in the programming room or the proposal room, whether it's at 6 a.m. or 6 p.m., I always see this gentleman working away at a fast pace. And that, gentlemen, is what I call a real NCR man!" Mr. Graham then gave me $100 in cash, which was a lot of money in those days, and his words and gesture were greeted with much applause. It's peculiar that Mr. Graham never asked me about my great tan; perhaps it was an oversight not to ask him to go sailing that weekend, but he taught me a lesson in life—one about perception and reality.

By all means, marry.
If you get a good wife,
you'll become happy;
if you get a bad one,
you'll become a philosopher.

Socrates

3-bravo
My Virgin E-mail and Judge Lucy

Western 29, my airline ticketing company, was highly innovative and the first company to do airline ticketing, itineraries, invoices and other associated applications for the travel industry. In fact, Western 29 was the first company outside of the airline industry to offer airline ticketing to travel agents.

Around 1976, about a year after a subsidiary of McDonald-Douglas bought Western 29, we were attending the annual travel industry international convention in Madrid, Spain. We were displaying our new system, "Post Office,"[15] in a large pavilion at the convention center when someone from airline ticketing screamed out to me, "Mr. Brent, you have a post office message." My only response to this incredible statement was, "Really?" After asking her to explain it to me, we sat down on the sixth step of the pavilion and read the following message, sent from my office at the Cathedral Hill Hotel, San Francisco –

QUOTE - An officer of the San Francisco Police Department by the name of Tom Moloney was here today to arrest you for $1,640 in parking tickets in

---

[15] A forerunner to today's e-mail (absolutely the same format and style).

the City & County of San Francisco. He said he would
check with me later and wanted to know where you
were. We told him you were in Madrid. What shall
we tell him? END-QUOTE

Following a moment of guilt-ridden reflection on my path, we
replied,

QUOTE Please tell Officer Moloney that I will be back
on the 16th and at that time, I will drop by the Hall of
Justice and surrender myself for the parking tickets.
END-QUOTE

The day after returning to San Francisco, a seemingly levelheaded
Officer Moloney received assurance that I would resolve the situation.
To prove that Officer Moloney had contacted me, an event which
subsequently resulted in an appearance at the Hall of Justice on the
eighth floor, a policeman took one thumbprint.[16] Officer Moloney
informed me, "Tomorrow, you have to go to traffic court. Go tell your
story, and with any kind of extenuating circumstances at all, they'll
usually waive some of the penalties and interest. And, the judge is
pretty cool; she's younger than most judges and seems to cut a pretty
fair deal for most people." Then he said, "I think you'll do okay."

It seemed like a good idea to present myself in a humble and sincere
manner at court the following day. A never-worn, polyester brown
suit that had seemed to be a foolish purchase made in Houston, Texas,

---

[16] How embarrassing to have only one fingerprint taken; the really serious guys get all of
the fingerprints!

a few years earlier became my court attire. The brown suit resembled a basic bookkeeper's uniform; when it was paired with an old shirt

and simple tie, the basic bookkeeper look became me!

Judge Lucy Kelly McCabe's courtroom was a full house the next morning. After 45 minutes of watching her, it was apparent she had both a sense of humor and discernment as she dispensed mercy to some and penalties to others.

After nearly an hour, the court clerk—a very severe-sounding, African-American woman—called out, "BRENT!" Immediately, the hulking African-American gentleman, who had been seated next to me, bolted to his feet in tandem with my movements. My reaction was, "I think she meant me." He countered with, "No, no, it's for me!" Who was a smallish Irishman to argue with a guy who probably played linebacker in middle school? So, he got an "okay" from me.

Judge McCabe was looking at some giant 11x16 page printouts as the linebacker approached the bench. She asked him rhetorically, "You're Brent?" And he replied, "Yes, Your Honor." Judge McCabe rephrased her question, "You're Patrick Timothy Brent?" To this very direct question, the linebacker corrected himself with, "No, no, I'm Grant." The opportunity to correct this blunder had arrived; I walked up behind Mr. Grant, gave a little wave, and humbly said, "I think that's for me." Judge McCabe offered us a half-smile, and Mr. Grant returned to his seat. To lighten the moment, I quipped, "For a minute I thought I had a long-lost relative." That remark earned me a good chuckle from everyone in the courtroom, including Judge McCabe . . . everyone except the clerk, who drilled holes into me with her eyes for a moment.

When the laughter died down, Judge McCabe gave me her full attention. "You ought to get an award. You have the largest number of tickets of anyone we've had here in several weeks," she said as she flipped through page after page of my traffic violation history spanning three or four years. The judge found one report particularly interesting and questioned me about it:

"What's this one where you got both a parking ticket and a moving violation for a car you weren't physically occupying at the time? The report indicates this occurred in front of the St. Francis Hotel on Post Street. It seems like your car was not parked quite right, and it rolled into a bus. The police had to put it back into position, and they gave you several tickets."

How was she to know my response would be classically Irish?

"Oh, I always wondered what happened to the rubber molding

on my old blue Mercedes."

She continued browsing my history, mentioned a few other tickets, and finally said, "The total is $1,640." Looking at me, she continued, "Well, we can probably waive some of the interest to get it down." After conferring with the clerk, she offered, "We can maybe get this down to $860." After another conference with the clerk, she asked me, "How does $560 sound?" In an effort to stay in character as a "basic bookkeeper," I just looked at her, cringed a little, and said nothing. At this point, the conferring between judge and clerk had escalated to a heated discussion. Finally, Judge McCabe gave me her best offer: "Mr. Brent, how does $140 sound? And, if you need it, we can give you a payment schedule." My answer was, "I can handle that." She queried, "You can handle it now?" The bookkeeper in me calmly replied, "Yes, today."

Knowing what the situation could become, my back-up plan involved $2000 in cash, which was on my person. Quickly paying the $140, my last submission to "the court" was a "thank-you" note for the judge. The next day, Judge McCabe called and invited me to lunch at Hamburger Mary's. After our lunch date, she would occasionally invite me to dinner. A divorcée with a couple of kids, Lucy McCabe was a little older than me. We became friends but never really dated. A while later, she and a gentleman friend attended my annual St. Patrick's Day party. Before leaving the event, Lucy told me, "If I had known anything about you . . . your corporation, your home, your polo playing . . . I probably wouldn't have given you the verdict I did, Patrick."

It *was* St. Patrick's Day, and with a twinkle in my eye, the Irishman in me replied, "I suspected that, too." The reality of the situation is that the bookkeeper brown suit was not intended to deceive; my humblest suit facilitated an accurate perception of a man humbled by the sudden gravity of his circumstances.

This legal saga of mine has a small, subsidiary story attached that involved my friends, Jay and Judy Cassell. Judy was one of those people who thought that my life was a little too blessed. During this time, when traffic tickets were accumulating, Jay and I did a 15-mile run to their home in Sausalito at least three times a week. On the evenings that we ran, Jay and Judy would come to my office around 1700, and Judy would drive my Mercedes to their house for me. Afterwards, we'd share a light dinner.

During one of our dinners, Jay and Judy heard the story of the $1,600 in parking tickets and my upcoming court date. "Oh, that's terrible, Patrick!" Judy's response did not sound exactly sincere, and the slight smirk on her face revealed her inner thoughts. Later, during a long run with Jay, my suspicions were confirmed when he remarked, "Judy really thinks it's about time somebody gave you a good thrashing for your outrageous behavior." Of course, they would be the first to know of such an event.

Jay and I were scheduled to run together on my court date. After my extremely successful encounter with the judge, they came by the office for Judy to fetch the car, as usual. As we began our run to Sausalito, he immediately asked, "What happened in court? Tell me about it." When he heard the full story, he exclaimed, "Oh, Judy is not going to like that at all." The Irishman in me suggested an alternative: "Well, Judy doesn't have to hear that. What do you think she'd like to hear?" During our long trek across the Golden Gate Bridge and up and down the hills of Marin toward his house, we decided to give Judy another version of the story. After showering, the three of us went out for dinner. Judy couldn't wait to ask what happened in court. She had no way to know about my conversation with Jay, and so the story was told like this:

"Well, it sure wasn't my best day. The judge told me I was outrageous and arrogant, and threw the book at me for the full amount—plus some other penalties and things of that nature."

With that same satisfied little smirk on her face, Judy sympathized, "Oh, Patrick, that's really, really too bad. I'm sorry." On our next run, Jay gave me a rundown of Judy's reaction. "You really made her day! She was so happy that your life received a certain amount of grief. She said it gave the world balance."

In six months' time, Jay and Judy attended the same St. Patrick's Day party that Lucy McCabe attended. Over the course of the evening, Judy met the judge. Naturally, one of the most common questions at my parties was, "How do you know Patrick?" When Judy posed this question, the judge replied that our meeting had occurred upon the occasion of an appearance in her courtroom for traffic violations. When the Cassells went home that night, Judy queried Jay, "Are you sure that was the judge who really threw the book at him? Why would he have her at the St. Patrick's Day party?" Jay replied, "Beats me!"

To this day, Judy has her version of my story, a view of me that preserves our relationship; and then, there is reality.

Flattery is all right,
as long as one doesn't inhale.

Fred Dailey

30 June 1982

3-charlie
Dynamite

During a holiday season long ago, my Thanksgiving plans involved a date with a young lady and a rendezvous in the Bahamas. Upon my arrival in Nassau a day or two early, the news came that in spite of all of my arrangements, the young lady would not be making the trip. That evening found me dressed in a white dinner jacket, making the best of the situation by playing roulette and chatting with a few ladies. The next day, it was on to Ft. Lauderdale for a few days of sunshine before making the trip back to the Windy City.

The Queen Elizabeth the First—that grand old ship—was the newest attraction in Port Everglades, Florida, and a tour of the vessel sounded most appealing. As luck would have it,[17] a former Miss Florida was in charge of the tour, and she guided my group around the ship. Miss Jolly McCall was a strikingly attractive young lady with an hourglass figure, auburn hair, and a few well-placed freckles that appeared to dance at times. Her failure to notice me prompted my efforts to ask a few more questions than anyone else on the tour, as is my style. Still, her attention was not lingering on me. When we

---

[17] Maybe it wasn't luck; maybe it happened through a machination on my part . . .

arrived at the bridge, a giant sign with "GMT" in big, bold letters hung above the ship's clock. Our tour guide had overlooked a few of my other questions, but at least she recognized me as the guy who asked all the questions. Here was my chance to impress her.

I asked our tour guide what GMT meant. She turned red and replied, "I'm not sure. Maybe I'll find out later." Here is how I explained it to her in front of the crowd: "Well, if everyone would like to know, it means 'Greenwich Mean Time.' It's the way all pilots, ship captains and navigators set their clocks by a village named Greenwich just east of London, England." Somehow, between my question and my answer, the "guy who asked all the questions" became memorable to our tour guide, and my reward was probably what Hawaiians would call a grand "stink-eye"! Jolly McCall wasn't going to forget me for a long time to come.[18]

My immediate efforts to be charming and to make up for showing off didn't work on Jolly; she made it very clear that my personage was persona-non-grata. At the end of the tour, three dozen white roses were dispatched to Jolly from me. It was a long shot, but she was quite an attractive young lady.

About 1830 hours that night, the phone rang in my hotel room; Jolly McCall was calling to tell me that the roses were grand, but I was not. However, life marches on. Years later, we shared a Mardi Gras in New Orleans, and over the course of many other ventures,

---

[18] Jolly McCall was our tour guide's name.

including meeting her and her new husband in Chicago, we became lifelong friends. There was the time that my friend Nick Calvert and I rented a Comanche aircraft that was malfunctioning in an increasingly worrisome way, but we successfully flew Jolly and her equally attractive girlfriend to lunch in Freeport, Bahamas. When we couldn't get the plane to work, Nick turned himself upside down, crawled underneath—where all the electronics were located, and pushed the radio back up to make it work. We took off from Ft. Lauderdale with no more trouble. At the end of our 45-minute flight to Freeport, Nick went upside down again to push the radio up again; I hailed the tower, and we landed. What a jaunt we had that day! In fact, Jolly and her girlfriend called our trip "dynamite." She rightly considered me out of line the day we met, but overall, it seems one is often remembered for being outrageous but rarely recovers from anonymity.

Volume II

GENTLEMAN

*Never enter a room without improving
the situation before you leave.*

Nick Calvert

13 July 1972

This tree in front of the National Museum of the
Marine Corps is dedicated to Nick Calvert. The web
address for the National Museum of the Marine
Corps is www.usmcmuseum.org.

Shibumi

a state of effortless perfection

Just prior to my 25th birthday, I met Nick Calvert, a former U.S. Navy submariner who would later become my roommate, role model and lifelong friend. To me, he epitomized the Japanese term, "Shibumi," which represents a natural sense of graciousness, a balance of simplicity and complexity. Of the many things Nick Calvert taught me, none is more important than this principle: it is not how much money you have or how many assets you acquire; it is how you behave, how you comport yourself, how you do the little things in life. Fred Astaire knew and practiced this principle. Everything was always perfection in his movies and in his environment. Style and form are everything. Nick taught me the practical measures and the discipline behind this type of diligence that seems so effortless to the world once it's learned. He taught me how to set a gig line,[19] how to wear a hat, the manner in which clothes should be cleaned, the way to square everything away, the

---

[19] **Gig line** is a military term that refers to the edge of one's shirt, belt buckle, and trouser fly. In order to be properly dressed, these three should align to form a straight line down the front of a person's body.
The name derives from the use of the word "gig" to mean a violation or infraction during inspection. Unpolished brass, unshined shoes, and sloppy gig lines are all "gigs." From "Gig Line," Wikipedia, accessed 24 February 2010.

reason for wearing long-sleeved shirts, how to use a napkin, and why and how a man should partially rise each and every time a lady leaves the dining table. In short, he taught me how to be a gentleman. All of these seemingly small things add up to make life better for you and the people who surround you.

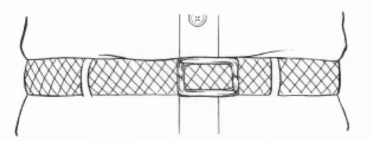

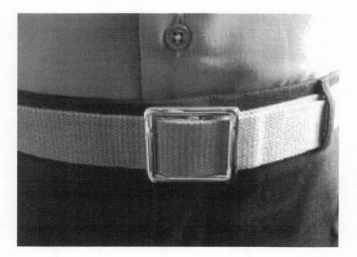

4
Nicholas Peter Calvert, United States Navy

First of all, it should be said that everyone needs a Nick Calvert in his life. Unfortunately, there are damn[20] few gentlemen of his quality in the world. It was my good fortune to meet him just prior to my 25th birthday. My six-year career in the Marine Corps Reserve was wrapping up, and about the same time, Nick Calvert was finishing up a five and a half-year stint as an electronics technician and a former submariner with the United States Navy. We met in a pub in Chicago. The dental supply salesman who was supposed to be my roommate in my new condominium wasn't quite ready to move in, and Nick Calvert was a combination of Bob Hope, Johnny Carson and Errol Flynn rolled into one guy. Nick was everything that I was not. He had a personality and a love of life that was second to none. Needless to say, the dental supply salesman was gently phased out, and Nick Calvert became my roommate and co-mischief maker.

Three stewardesses lived across from my condo, and the four of us had become spiritual friends. They wanted to pass judgment on

---

[20] Originally, this sentence said, "very few," but the author deferred to a more experienced writer's advice: "Substitute *damn* every time you're inclined to write *very*; your editor will delete it and the writing will be just as it should be." **Mark Twain**

my incoming roommate. Nick came over to the apartment, and we played a game of chess. Afterwards, we strolled over to the girls' home for introductions and drinks. Around 2200 hours, this recently discharged Marine Reservist went home. Nick stayed with the girls to have one more drink. About 0930 hours the next morning, I was at work and called the girls to get their opinion. "Well, what do you think? Should we accept Nick Calvert? What do you have to say about him?" One of those stewardesses replied, "Oh we think he's just grand. Do you want to talk to him? He's still here." Nick was more handsome and more popular with women than his future roommate ever would be.

Nick and I sailed and flew airplanes together, and he could not have been a better copilot or first mate on the sailboat. He could go into Butch McGuire's Pub and emerge with a handful of girls to come with us for a day of yachting. When we had a six-passenger plane through the charter outfit, Nick would go to pubs and try to sell four of the seats—usually to young ladies—for a trip to the Bahamas with one gas stop. Little did they know that the flight would take about 10 hours, but they all signed on at $50 per person. Meigs Airport—the one we used—was located downtown and was surrounded by water on three sides. So, with Lake Michigan splashing onto the runway, our plane would take off... very much like an aircraft carrier. Our flight plan was basic: we flew out of Meigs Airport, refueled in Atlanta, and went straight to the Bahamas. We never socialized with any of these ladies, but it certainly made for a great life when our money was at a minimum. In fact, with second-hand tuxedos and a whole bunch of contacts in the hotel business, Nick and I applied our entire methodology of living the good life with very little money, and we succeeded.

Later on, Joe Penar popped up again and wanted me to go in with him to buy an old, rusted Cessna 172. He abandoned the airplane in Jacksonville, Florida, when the weather got bad, even though I had signed a contract to buy half of the plane. Nick and I wanted to go get it, so we convinced the girls[21] across from the swimming pool to give us one-way youth fare tickets[22] down to Jacksonville. We found the airplane, got some charts, and found someone to jumpstart it for us. At the time, I had only 50 hours of flight time and only one test night landing. (By this time, it was midnight.) We had some trouble tuning in the radio frequencies, but we finally found one from the tower; and they gave us a clearance. We took off toward the east, and not being quite confident at that time on navigation, we saw a black abyss ahead. Nick identified that as the Atlantic Ocean and figured that we should go to the right (south).

We had planned to spend the weekend in Nassau, because we certainly didn't want to rush home with our new airplane. Turning south, we counted the airport beacons because we couldn't make radio contact. When we got to West Palm Beach, which is parallel

---

[21] my stewardess neighbors and spiritual friends
[22] Technically, one had to be 19 years old or younger to fly on a youth fare ticket.

to the Bahamas, we landed without a clearance . . . in the dark . . . at about 0400. After talking to Butler Aviation of Chicago O'Hare fame, they got a few frequencies working about eight hours later; we jury-rigged everything we could and took off for the Bahamas. We had a lot of trouble with navigation. Crabbing an airplane into the wind was not part of my skill set at the time, so we kept blowing farther and farther south. All the while, we thought that we were going straight east, making adjustments, toward Cuba.

Finally, when we were about halfway there, I figured it out, but our flight had consumed a lot of valuable fuel. About 20 minutes out of Nassau, the sky was becoming impossibly dark, and we could barely make out a runway in a fishing village below on an island called Andros. We were almost out of fuel, but when I mentioned to Nick that we should land on Andros and hope for the best, he refused. Nick said to me, "Well, this airport has no fuel, and we don't want to spend Saturday night in a fishing village. Let's keep going." We charged ahead. By that time, we had learned navigation and were on a straight course. We found an old, battered chart with a penciled-in mark, which was a frequency, and promptly dialed Nassau tower. A guy with a proper Bahamian accent came aboard and welcomed 5836 Alfa for a "straight-in" approach to Runway 5. We landed and taxied up to a red carpet, which is routine there, even for humble private planes (and none were as humble as ours). On the red carpet, we were welcomed by some local girls with Bacardi rum punches and some guys playing calypso music—a customary greeting for each and every airplane that came in. We stayed at the Royal Victoria Hotel[23] which reminded us of the Royal Hawaiian. For two days, we reveled in the Bahamas—as much as any two sailors would. When they fueled the plane two days after our arrival, we found out that we had only 16 minutes of fuel left when we landed! The next morning, we stopped in Miami, saw Nick's folks, and took off for Chicago. This is where we really became veterans.

For January, the weather was icy, snowy and cold. We refueled in many places along our trip home. We even had to hedge-hop at times. Before we reached Tupelo, Mississippi, the plane started icing up. We made a quasi-emergency landing in Tupelo because ice broke off

---

[23] a grand old place that is now unfortunately ruined

the plane.[24] We dried off the plane and refueled before continuing our mission in the midst of the bad weather. Please note that we never gave up a mission—which is one reason why females are better pilots than men. To most men, the flight is the "mission." For most women, the flight is a "safety issue," which is far, far smarter. We said to the fuel purveyor in Tupelo, "God, we almost died here in Mississippi, or at least in the sky above you. What a place to go!" The fuel purveyor assured us that Tupelo wouldn't have been a bad spot to conclude the ultimate journey. "This is a famous town," he said. "Don't you know Elvis Presley was born here?" That afforded us some small degree of solace.

From Tupelo, we proceeded to work our way northward. Finally, we made it into Lombard, Illinois, to Mitchell Field, where there was no instrument approach. Not that it would have mattered; we had no instrument rating anyway. So, we shot a VOR[25] approach into DuPage County, followed Highway 64 North Avenue until we got to an outdoor theatre we knew, and then picked up a heading north-northwest into the threshold, all above the one, tiny runway this airport had. We spotted the runway and put her down. During the entire flight home, we were only 200-300 feet above the ground because it was heavily IFR (Instrument Flight Rules), which is clearly not the way to fly. With my instrument and commercial ratings, the

---

[24] That would not be the last time this would happen in my aviation pursuits.
[25] Very High Frequency Omnirange

years that followed would bring safer planes with much improved avionics. This, however, did not prevent many misadventures.

Some people wonder all their lives
if they've made a difference.
Marines don't have that problem.

Ronald Reagan

17 March 1985

Chapter 5 is dedicated to Don Reid and Chuck Vogt, two all wet Leathernecks who tutored the author (later to become a "one-time" life member of the infamous San Francisco Dolphin club) in transiting San Francisco's cold bay with just goggles and a speedo--bravo zulu-- originally a "boot" to rough water. Lock 'n' load, Jarheads.

5
Big Buck

All of us have those exceptional people in our lives—people who are outrageous or in some way remarkable—and altogether unforgettable. Such was the case with Colonel Buck Swannack—aka Big Buck.

In San Francisco, at 0900 hours every Sunday, the Dolphin South-End Running Club (DSE Runners) meets. Their logo, which they wear proudly on their garish orange T- shirts, features a turtle and the club motto, "Start Slow and Taper Off."

At the time of my involvement with the DSE Runners, approximately 200 people met every single Sunday and ran a different scenic trip, anywhere from a mile and a quarter to 10 miles. Early on in my years in San Francisco, I was lured back into a proper running program and ran as a member of this particular club. One of our more boisterous members was a fellow named Buck Swannack. Whenever Buck was around, wherever we were running, he was "the show." At 6'2," and with a shaved head, Buck used any excuse to show off his powerful chest. He claimed to be a veteran Marine combat colonel, and he was larger than life. Clearly, Buck Swannack was not "my kind of guy."

Avoiding Buck became a regular activity during our club runs. Well into the winter season, when we were running at the "Great Beach" along the Cliff House,[26] Buck marched up to me and said, "I've decided I'm running with you today. Your name's Pat, right?" Taking into consideration my opinion of Buck, I merely replied, "To what do I owe this honor?" Buck was undeterred. "I just found out that you're a Marine . . . a jarhead . . . a Leatherneck . . . my kind of guy." Just before that remark, he commented, "I used to think you were just some kind of ordinary slob like all these other runners, but you're a Marine. Since we're both Marines, we're going to run together." My only response to this stunning compliment was, "Well . . . thanks."

Buck's impromptu authority was seldom challenged. Thus was the start of my long, albeit reluctant, relationship with this extraordinary individual. Buck came to all my events. He attended two of my St. Patrick's Day parties at San Francisco City Hall and a St. Patrick's Day polo event, and he showed up at an airplane hangar where some of my other parties were held. For eight years running, Buck came out to the desert for the Governor's Ball I hosted. He wore many versions of formal wear, but usually finished his ensemble with a kilt. Here is a little snapshot of the kind of fellow Buck was: If he attended a men's luncheon, he would climb up on the table (in his kilt) and walk amongst the dishes and food while addressing all of the men about their general lack of character and how they should show more resolve and behave more like the U.S. Marines. Truly,

---

[26] Not too far from my residence at the time

Buck was a memorable one of a kind!

We ran together in the Tucson, Boston, and New York marathons. Everywhere Buck saw me—anywhere in the world—he would acknowledge me, because he considered me "his pal."[27] Buck finally married a lovely lady named Agnes from the Philippines and moved to Houston. We stayed in touch by telephone or through running club newsletters. Then, one day, there was a different kind of call from Buck. He wanted to let me know he was checking out. He was battling some type of cancer, and doctors had given him about four months to live. His good friend, Jimmy Anderson from Tucson, had flown there to take care of him, along with Agnes. By this time, we are well into the 1980s. Over a period of more than 25 years, fondness and a true admiration had developed in my heart for this gentleman who had more than his share of hubris.

As a final gesture to my dear friend, a Marine Corps general, who happened to be the commandant at the time, graciously granted my request to draft a letter. Since the Marines were Buck's all-time

---

[27] All because he thought it was cool to be a Marine.

favorite outfit (good choice), the letter would thank Buck for being a great American and a Marine kind of guy, recognizing that he was fighting a life-challenging battle, and acknowledging that he would handle it with the style and class of America's fighting men.

The commandant went for the idea, enhanced my letter, put it into a beautiful red binder, and shipped it off to a brand new second lieutenant in the Marine Corps who was visiting his mother in Houston that week. A newly minted second lieutenant named Tom Prentice hand-carried this letter to Buck's home in Houston and presented it to him. Anyone who knew Buck would understand that the letter represented the finest thing he could ever receive. His wife, Agnes, and friend, Jimmy, said it overwhelmed him. He called to thank me. At that time, he had only about a week left to live.

And this is where everything took a turn, and life reversed itself on me. My quiet inner thoughts turned to pride for my part in a good deed—as good a deed as one could do for a man like Buck. It was heartwarming to think of Buck's shipping off with such a great honor. During our years together, we had exchanged other awards and acknowledgements, but none at this level.

About 10 days later, on 13 December 1995, Buck Swannack died. Once again, while praying for Buck's soul, the letter, which his wife said she would frame and treasure forever, sprang to mind.

Soon after, another letter arrived at my daughter Laura's house. At the time, Laura was only about 2 years old. Her mother wept over the words she read to me over the telephone. Handwritten on a yellow legal pad, the sentiments were clearly a painstaking effort for the writer. The two-page letter told Laura Monaghan Brent what kind of guy Big Buck thought her father was. It was noble, honorable, and a staggering personal effort by a Marine kind of guy: Buck Swannack.

It took years for me to recover from this letter. Buck had successfully upstaged me, but so be it. I am forever in his debt.

In 1995, a few weeks after Lt. Tom Prentice delivered a very special letter from the commandant of the Marines Corps to Buck in Houston, he passed away. After he passed away, this letter arrived for Laura Brent, my 8-year-old daughter.

Dear Laura,

I am writing this letter to thank you for sharing your father with me. You came to our wedding in Pacifica, and then Aggie and I moved to Texas where we went on day trails. Your father and I have known each other for over a quarter of a very good century. I want to share some things with you he'd never talk about. Patrick has helped many, many a boy and man—and woman—to be the most that they can be. Most of these people simply don't understand that they stand a bit taller and more confident of themselves. Your dad told most of them the things he did and the favors he asked friends to do to make a person feel better about themselves. I am a better person for running with Patrick on many DSE runs when my anger over someone would spill out. After the run, I thought maybe that wasn't so bad after all. Your father had the ability to talk to me when other men would have feared me and not have said a word to me on my dark days.

I am now in my happy days living my life with the love of my life, Aggie, and longtime friend, Jimmy, who make each day a blessing.

Your dad and I met in Japan at the airport. I was on my way to climb Mt Fuji. Instead, I did it the easy way in the summer time. I climbed it and as the samurai say, "I looked the tiger in the eye and felt his breath." I was giving you this part about the tiger and Mt. Fuji so that your father will walk to the top of this famous mountain with you. When you are at the top, think about the old colonel running up nonstop at full speed at the top of the world and saying WAY TO BE!

Please excuse me for my penmanship, as I am losing a bit of my powers.

Take care of your dad for me,

Love,

Buck

P.T., right, with Buck and Linda at the 1978 Boston Marathon.

25 August 1995

Dear Buck,

It has come to my attention that you are facing significant medical challenges as of late.

Your many friends within the Marine Corps family have praised your dedication and contributions to our country and to the Corps over the years. These contributions have made it obvious to even the casual observer that you are the embodiment of the esprit de corps which we cherish so dearly.

On behalf of all Marines, I thank you for your years of dedicated effort and selfless contribution of time and energy.

Keep up the brave fight and know that our prayers are with you.

Semper Fidelis,

C.C. KRULAK
General, U.S. Marine Corps
Commandant of the Marine Corps

Mr. Buck Swannack
8206 Magnolia Glen
Humble, TX 77346

Letter to Buck from the Commandant of the Marine Corps,
General C.C. Krulak

Always forgive your enemies;
nothing annoys them so much.

Oscar Wilde

Chapter 6-alfa is dedicated to Crystal Long and Scarlett Hugentugler and the others who keep Patrick almost on the straight and narrow. Mahalo and fair winds.

6-alfa
Humor:
The Magic Ingredient

A constant belief of mine has been that humor is an important element of virtually everything in life. The most serious and emotional moments can be diffused and possibly better navigated with a touch of humor. All of the really great leaders in business, the military and politics have one thing in common—a reasonable and subtle form of humor as part of their composition.

Those who have been in middle management positions in my companies have heard my admonishments; when they have difficulty with an individual, their mission is to coach that person, humor him, and direct him. After about four to seven rounds of that scenario, they have to be bold enough and strong enough to terminate that person's employment. The majority of people can be rescued with coaching and humor. To that end, there have been many moments in my life that called for humor, with both loved ones and people who perhaps needed to know that they should not take me on unless they were ready for the consequences.

Glenn W. Schmidt was the finest boss anyone ever had and the gentleman who made a real businessman out of this Irishman. This man spent four and a half years with me at University Computing Company, where the stock went from zero to $189 a share, and then went down again to a dollar and a quarter after we left (no reflection on our departure). Glenn's sense of humor, intelligence and work ethic represented the epitome of a fine businessman. Like most people in top management positions, he did not realize his value. After rising to the executive level, he was never hesitant to go on a sales call or to work at the lowest, most basic level to get the job done. Most politicians, executives, priests, generals, governors and other highly successful people owe their successes to being just that—basically good, humble motivators—and a sense of humor is a bonus!

Glenn's wife, Carol, whom I dearly loved, always wanted to take me on. Perhaps that tendency could be traced to my first weekend visit to their home. The hour-long drive to Oak Lawn, Illinois, was an immediate deterrent, and Carol may not have liked hearing a blunt statement about that trip being the first and the last to said town. Suffice it to say, that promise has been kept all these years. From the beginning, Glenn saw me as a maverick kind of guy, but he wanted me to be a part of his organization. Glenn developed me with humor, leadership and discipline, using each at the appropriate time. Unlike Glenn, though, Carol had a hard time accepting me. It was not evident to me how the three of us were getting along until the company had a few layoffs and a guy named Joe told me, "Don't worry, Patrick, you'll never get laid off." That was hard to believe, so I asked, "Why would you say that?" Joe replied, "Because Glenn Schmidt thinks you are one of the coolest guys in the world." Surprised and relieved, my only response to him was, "You've got to be kidding!" Later, both Glenn and I transferred to Dallas and then to Houston in a string of promotions that usually belonged to gentlemen 30 years our senior.[28]

To my surprise, when Glenn and Carol had their third child, a son, they named him after me, Patrick Timothy Schmidt.[29] How he convinced Carol to name her third son after me is beyond my knowledge or imagination. True to his name, Patrick Timothy Schmidt is a fine young man, a dedicated Wisconsin highway patrolman, and a member of the sniper and SWAT team in Eagle River, Wisconsin. His hockey team calls him *kamikaze*.

There were other "children" that cemented my bond with the Schmidt family. On one occasion, they gave me a beagle named Bilbo. What followed was a series of beagles named Frodo Baggins, Chicago Baggins, and so forth. Each of the Baggins beagles lived to be 16, then passed away; they are buried together at Lake Merced, home of the Irish Sprint.[30]

My visits with my three calabash[31] nephews—Danny, David, and my namesake, Patrick Timothy—and my one calabash niece, Robyn, were very frequent, even though Carol said she didn't want them

---

[28] Both Glenn and I were in our 20s.
[29] That's the first time I realized that Glenn really thought well of me.
[30] The Irish Sprint has been a tradition since 1982; Deborah Neil is the force that made the Irish Sprint really work.
[31] In Hawaiian, calabash is an adopted relative, not necessarily of the same bloodline.

visiting me or learning any of my bad habits.

One of the things Carol forbade the children from having was a pool table. Much to her chagrin, a pool table sporting an engraving that read "From Uncle Patrick" appeared at the Schmidt residence for Christmas. Later, both Glenn and Carol thanked me for the pool table because they said it kept the boys off the streets during their teen years and gave them something to do with their friends in the winters. That pool table made their home the social focal point of the neighborhood, and much fun was had by all.

As time passed, each boy took his turn visiting me in San Francisco. While they were with me, they were introduced to cool-looking sport coats and casual dress. Their father, Glenn, was always kind of formal. My favorite joke and description of him was that his idea of getting comfortable after work was loosening his tie. I laughed picturing him lying in bed in a grey business suit.

Somehow, in the midst of our years together, a false rumor started that Uncle Patrick was a millionaire. During each of my trips to Naperville, Illinois, where the Schmidts were then living, seven or eight kids would get on their bicycles and ride around me in a circle during my jog around the neighborhood. It wasn't until much later that their motive was revealed; those kids simply wanted ride their bikes with the millionaire from Hawaii while he did his jogging.

Carol always left instructions for the boys when they were going to be with me. In spite of, or possibly because of, my passion for polo,[32] Carol told the boys that they were not permitted to play polo or to own a horse. Aha! Carol should have known me well enough to know what would happen next. My three nephews were going to be impressed by Uncle Patrick's latest caper.

Shortly thereafter, during a polo match at Oak Brook, which was just a few miles from Naperville, the opportunity for my prank arose. It was time to have some harmless fun with my friends, the Schmidts. Upon my instruction, Murphy, a polo trainer for Oak Brook, delivered a polo horse to the Schmidt residence. Christine[33] and I arrived early, intending to find Glenn and then surprise everyone. However, Glenn was already on the golf course with one of the boys, Danny. We went to the golf course and rented a cart; then we found Glenn and Danny and explained our hijinks. Of course, they wanted to be in on it, so the golf game was terminated, and we all went back to the house to hide out and wait for the fun to begin.

At exactly 1500 hours, a long trailer, that would normally hold 12 horses, pulled up in front of the Schmidts' very expensive residence in Naperville.[34] Then, the horse, all beautifully done in perfect polo style—polished and clean with white bandages on the legs—came up the driveway—a total non sequitur in this upscale neighborhood. *Cloop! Cloop! Cloop!* Murphy led the horse up to the gate, where Carol

---

[32] My life-long love of polo started in Hawaii with the help of Mike Dailey's father and Bob McGregor.

[33] Laura's (my daughter) mother

[34] Naperville is one of the really upscale communities with giant u-shaped driveways, where all of the "swells" live.

was waiting and handed her the lead line. He told her, "This is a gift for the boys from Uncle Patrick. In times to come, there will be more horses coming, and I hope you enjoy it." Murphy had been ordered to leave, regardless of the panic that might ensue. Carol turned around and demanded, "What are you doing? Come back here." Completely obedient to his instruction, Murphy just waved, got into the truck, and drove away. Her adrenaline level rising, Carol told Danny, who had emerged from the house, to call his "blankety-blank Uncle Patrick"[35] in San Francisco. Robyn was instructed to call her father at the office, the country club, or wherever he blankety-blank was located!

In the midst of Carol's mini-meltdown, Christine walked over and introduced herself, "I'm a new neighbor here. How come you have a horse in your driveway?" Through the side window, we could hear Carol telling her kids, "Get this dingbat lady out of here!" Carol was becoming extremely upset—so upset that it made me think my stunt was over the top. Then, my glance fell on Glenn. His eyes were tearing; his joy was unbounded. He was having one good time, so I said to Christine (who had slipped back

---

[35] The words Carol used to fill in the "blankety-blanks" were pretty bad that day!

into the house), "Let the good times roll!" Christine slipped back outside to question Carol. "Aren't there some zoning laws or something of that nature?" Carol responded hotly, "You've got to get out of here. Just leave me alone!" After watching Carol suffer through another 20 minutes or so of stress and panic over what to do with this 1,200-pound beast in her driveway, we emerged and revealed the joke. It was 1700 or 1800 hours, and many of the Schmidts' neighbors were arriving home from work. By and large, their neighbors were affluent executives who worked nearby at IBM and Bell Labs; and they wanted to see the horse and have their photos taken with it. All of a sudden, Carol went from being an extremely distressed housewife to being the neighborhood celebrity. People were having their pictures taken and riding around the lawn on the horse, when lo and behold, Mr. Murphy came back to retrieve it. After this prank of mine, Carol was a little more respectful of Uncle Patrick and doesn't mess around with him much to this day.

Basking in the glow of the success of my prank on Carol, we decided that Glenn had to have his turn. Glenn is not simply a conservative dresser; he is the most conservative, religious and faithful husband in the whole world. He used to make the facetious comment that "all he ever wanted in his life was a Swedish barmaid with an emotional problem." During Glenn's next visit to Palm Springs to play golf at the much-lauded PGA West, we decided to surprise him. Christine and others hired an actress with a great Swedish accent and a dynamite hourglass figure to play the part of the Swedish barmaid. This actress was very sexy and was often hired to imitate Marilyn Monroe. In the midst of a tornado watch,[36] we managed to videotape the entire episode ... the "Swedish barmaid" hugging Glenn and telling him that she was HIS Swedish barmaid. Glenn turned scarlet with embarrassment and tried to flee the scene. He did not succeed and ended up having a good time, but Carol does not like the story at all. Of course, the Irishman behind the prank and his cohorts in crime, Vern Churchill and the CEO of Glenn's company,[37] cherish the memory. The tale of a good practical—or impractical—joke tends to linger ...

For St. Patrick's Day each year, I hired some Stanford graduates to develop an outrageous corporation to do stunts at conventions and parties. Their annual challenge was to develop something that was exciting and showy, but never over the line. One year, they hired actors to pose as FBI agents who came into my St. Patrick's Day party and arrested one of my guests. Another year, they played a "Jeopardy" game in the rotunda at City Hall. All of the events they planned were memorable and hopefully, in good taste. Everyone received them well. In particular, everyone always enjoyed the belly dancers—or perhaps we just appreciate the arts more than most red-blooded men.

One of the most outrageous characters we encountered was "the bag lady." She actually was an attractive, middle-aged lady whose

---

[36] The tornado touched down just as we finished filming ...
[37] Glenn's company's name – Market Facts, Inc.

shtick was impersonating a down-and-out, yet brazen, bag lady. In many ways, she pranced around like the Eliza Doolittle character from *My Fair Lady*. We hired the "bag lady" to perform her routine with the manager of the polo club and several other people at various St. Patrick's Day parties, and hilarity was set in motion. One event involving the "bag lady" stands out as being the best evening ever. She made her appearance at a special dinner party hosted by the new commanding officer of the 12th Marine Corps District, Colonel Dick Camp, and his wife. The Camps have a lovely residence on Treasure Island, just outside of San Francisco. For their very first dinner party, they invited their commanding general from San Diego, Hugh Kerr, and his wife, Susan, as well as Christine and me.

The Camps wanted the evening to be perfect; it didn't turn out the way they planned. Toward the end of dinner, we heard a loud banging on the rear door of their home. The "bag lady" was outside, making a lot of noise and yelling in a loud Cockney accent, "You folks sure have a lot of great trash you're throwing away here in your garbage cans." To everyone's astonishment, she walked right into the house. What a sight she was—heavily made-up with big rouge cheeks, tattered clothes, and of course, about 10 shopping bags, overflowing with junk. The bag lady's lengthy discourse on the state of the Camps' garbage made the general quite uncomfortable. Dick Camp saw his career passing before him and ending before it had truly begun; but all three women were enjoying themselves, as was the sponsor of the spectacle.

Right before the bag lady made her exit, she turned to General Hugh Kerr and said, "I'm leaving soon. You're probably ready for me to go, right?" He kind of nodded. "Before I go, I want just one more thing, General." She took out a wrinkled paper bag, showed General Kerr it was empty, and gave him some instructions. "Put your left hand in here. Come on; just humor me. Now put your right hand in." Both of the general's hands were inside the bag. Then she looked at the general and said, "Now do it, General. Do it." He looked at her, not understanding; so she told him again, "General, I said, do it!" Perplexed, he asked her, "What do you mean? What do you mean?" Then, she just looked at him with her hands on her hips. "Wouldn't you know it? You get a Marine general in the sack, and he doesn't know what to do!"

Those who have fallen "victim" to my pranks have proven themselves to be great leaders, good sports and trusted friends.

KYEOTB.

P.T.B.'s Literary And Cinematic Recommendations For Major Tommy Prentice

Recently had dinner with a world-class gentleman who had never heard of "Ferris Bueller's Day Off"... remarkable; with that in mind...

BOOKS

Must reads or P.T.B. becomes bitter

Taipan
James Clavell (then the sequel)
Noble House
James Clavell
Wanderer
Sterling Hayden
Voyage
Sterling Hayden
Flags of our Fathers
John Bradley
Vicar of Christ
Walter F. Murphy
From Here to Eternity
James Jones

My Wicked, Wicked Ways:
the autobiography of Errol Flynn
  Errol Flynn and Jeffrey Meyers
The Princess Bride
  William Goldman
  (First, see the movie which did a fine job of
  following the book.)
The Corps (series)
  W.E.B. Griffin
Over the Edge of the World:
Magellan's Terrifying Circumnavigation
of the Globe
  Laurence Bergreen

MOVIES

"Darling Lili"
  PTB's all-time favorite movie—WWI era: war,
  romance and awesome music by Julie Andrews
"Start the Revolution Without Me"
  Gene Wilder and Donald Sutherland . . . gets even
  better after the 29th viewing
"South Pacific"
  Best musical ever made; new generations have never
  seen it. (Laura watched it four times the first week
  she saw it.)

"From Here to Eternity"
   after the book has been read
"Sands of Iwo Jima"
   John Wayne
"Red River"
   Best western ever made—John Wayne and
   Montgomery Clift
"Yankee Doodle Dandy"
   with James Cagney; nominated for 1942 Academy
   Award for best picture
"The Princess Bride"
   after the book has been read
"To the Shores of Tripoli"
   John Payne and Maureen O'Hara in her redheaded
   prime
"The Quiet Man"
   Maureen O'Hara and John Wayne (their personal
   favorites); filmed in Ireland
"Ferris Bueller's Day Off"
   Chicago based; a classic
"Song of the Islands"
   Betty Grable's Irish film in Hawaii
"Full Metal Jacket"
   Caution: first half only; second half depressing
"Fantasia"
   Disney classic with fantastic music

"Easter Parade"
  Fred Astaire and Judy Garland
"Casablanca"
  Bogart and Bergman
"Knute Rockne All American"
  with the Gipper Ronald Reagan and Pat O'Brien
"Rudy"
  a Notre Dame classic
"San Francisco"
  Clark Gable and Jeanette MacDonald
"Moonstruck"
  a warm Italian classic
"The Sheepman"
  Glenn Ford (former 1942 Marine)
"Second Hand Lions"
  classic with Robert Duvall and Michael Caine
"Hollywood and the Marines"
  for Devil Pups fundraiser starring TSOCP & PTB
  who introduced journey through Marine Corps via
  Hollywood film clips
"Lonely are the Brave"
  Kirk Douglas's best movie with his horse
"Whiskey"

Oscar Wilde's plays and movies: all of them

Noel Coward's plays and movies: all of them

There is something about
the outside of a horse
that is good for
the inside of a man.

Winston Churchill

Chapter 6-bravo is dedicated to Elizabeth Caselton whose determination and intelligence helped launch the new website PoloCollege.com for all those incorrigible polo types; thanks, Dr. Harris, too, & KYEOTB.

6-bravo
POLO

an exploration of glamour, style, danger and speed

One of my greatest "discoveries" was undoubtedly the sport of polo. If dynamite could be described as graceful, those references would surely apply.

During my stint as governor of the United States Polo Association (USPA), my favorite piece of counsel was that every handsome player in our club must wear a face guard. It's amazing that some players found that advice imposing—almost a sign of zealous authority. Sadly, there were two gentlemen—one from the Philippines and one from California—who became quadriplegics, paralyzed from the neck down by a tumble with a thoroughbred horse, performing at full speed.

Why does this sport hold such allure? One reason: it is breathtaking.

Imagine commanding a 1200-pound horse at full speed in an attempt to maneuver a ball the size of a baseball 300 meters to a goal, while your opponent can hook your mallet or ride directly into your side.

"Playing polo is like trying to play golf during an earthquake."
Anonymous

Polo created a way of life for me, a life that included two ranches, 14 horses and membership or ownership in two clubs. My training regimen was severe—particularly since I was a businessman with a full schedule.

Winston Churchill once said, "Polo is your passport to the world," and that statement certainly was validated for P.T. Brent. I've had the privilege of playing worldwide . . . a highlight would have to be Argentina which boasts some truly outstanding gentlemen; one was a Notre Dame Irishman from France! Coming from inner-city Chicago and having zero horse knowledge, it was quite an experience to arrive in Hawaii on business for my airline-ticketing computer company. There, two outstanding World War II gentlemen, Bob MacGregor and Fred Dailey—both world-class, old school players—introduced me to what is probably the world's greatest game. Later, I spoke as a eulogist at their funerals. Eleven of my polo acquaintances were killed on the polo pitch. And they say I am arrogant for calling for the face guard . . . amazing.

Unfortunately, the veterans are fading away, and many of the new players enter the sport solely for status. Drugs and spoiled lifestyles reign supreme for many polo enthusiasts.

The practice of hiring a professional now dominates the game at all levels.

The virtues and the discipline that once ruled may now be fading away.

However, we will be watching the next generation. For this poloist, the time has come to hang up the mallets . . . post multiple concussions, broken wrists, broken feet and countless contusions. All that remains are world-class memories, as well as a modicum of humility.

So now, focus, Mickey Britain . . .

KYEOTB.

> "They call it [polo] a gentleman's game
> for the same reason they call a tall man *Shorty*."
> Will Rogers

POLO: THE GAME OF KINGS

Polo is considered the oldest recorded team sport in known history, with the first polo matches recorded in 600 BC. Initially thought to have been created by competing tribes of Central Asia, it was quickly taken up as a training method for the King's elite cavalry. During the time when mounted armies swept back and forth across this part of the world, conquering and re-conquering, polo was adopted as the most noble of pastimes by the kings and emperors, sultans, shahs, caliphs and khans of the ancient Persians, Arabs, Mughals, Mongols and Chinese. It was for this reason it became known across the lands as "the game of kings."

British officers re-invented the game in 1862 and introduced it to England in 1869. Seven years later, sportsman James Gordon Bennett imported it to the United States.

BASIC RULES

The Line of the Ball

The most basic concept in the sport of polo is the line of the ball, a right-of-way established by the path of a traveling ball.

When a player has the line of the ball on his right, he has the right of way. This can be taken away by moving the player off the line of the ball by making shoulder-to-shoulder contact.

A player can:

hook an opponent's mallet

push him off the line

bump him with his horse

or steal the ball from him.

1 - The umpires' primary concerns are right-of-way and the line of the ball.

2 - The line of the ball is an imaginary line that is formed each time the ball is struck.

3 - This line traces the ball's path and extends past the ball along that trajectory.

4 - The player who last struck the ball is considered

to have right-of-way, and no other player may cross the line of the ball in front of that player.

5 - Riding alongside to block or hook is allowed, as long as the player with right-of-way is not impeded.

Ride Offs

Bumping or riding off is allowed as long as the angle of attack is less than 45 degrees, and any contact must be made between the pony's hip and shoulder.

Hooks

A player may hook or block another player's mallet with his mallet, but no deliberate contact between players is allowed. A player may not purposely touch another player, his tack or pony with his mallet.

Safety

The mallet may only be held in the right hand.

Left-handed players are often thought to hit with less accuracy, but guide their ponies better than their right-handed peers.

Do not mess with me, Frankie;
it will force the earth out of orbit
and we will plummet into the sun.

P.T.B.

7-alfa

Remedial Action

L ong ago, on a sunny afternoon in Chicago, before there were moon flights, my pals joined me for an afternoon around the pool in front of my condo at Executive Estates, close to O'Hare Field. One of the guys, Joe Penar, was bragging about his new private pilot's license and his 50 percent ownership in a Cessna Skyhawk 172. In front of a couple of attractive stewardesses, including one named Ann Hudson, Joe promised to fly all of us to the Montreal Expo, in the summer, for the World's Fair.[38] Of course, we all were enthused about the trip, and we waited and waited. Summer came and summer went; and Mr. Penar failed to keep his promise. It seemed that good old Joe went without Annie or me.

Needless to say, it was time for action. My temporary engagement with a company called General Dynamics was fading away and gave me quite a few extra hours for a boondoggle, which amounted to my venturing up to Sally's Flying School at Palwaukee Airport and deciding to do the whole nine yards—far more than Mr. Penar had undertaken. John Byers, my flight instructor at Sally's Flying School, was an all-American guy, and became my roommate and a lifelong

---

[38] The World's Fair that was taking place in Montreal in the late 1960s

friend. Eventually, he landed a job with a commercial charter outfit. However, before any of that happened, we launched plans for me to obtain my instrument rating. Two hundred hours later—more or less—after a lot of great adventures, that goal was achieved. By that time, John was working for a charter outfit called ATR at DuPage County Airport near Chicago. That's when the fun really began!

John and his friends at ATR helped me procure my commercial pilot's rating. These guys flew commercial flights and charters. Whenever they had more flights scheduled than pilots available, they let me fly a few of them. In the process of doing some occasional flying for ATR, the opportunity arose for me to lease an airplane through them. It was an ownership-lease of a Cherokee Piper Arrow—a high performance, single engine, retractable gear airplane.

In the meantime, my new career at University Computing Company was charging ahead, and Glenn Schmidt[39] and I were using the plane to fly all over the globe to do business deals. One time, we even landed at the Naval Ammunition Depot. Two Marine guards came out and blocked off the highway with railroad crossing guards. We landed on the highway, taxied onto a grass strip, and went to our meeting. Our escapades were always of this ilk. Once in Wisconsin, we landed right on the grass to go to a meeting in FonDuLac.

When my flight logbook was reading 700+ hours, Glenn and I

---

[39] the best boss a guy ever had

decided to take one of our customers to Vail for some skiing. The ski trip was successful, and fortunately for Al Grenlie, he flew home on a commercial flight instead of returning with us. We left a very snowy and foggy Denver airport to return to Chicago with one gas stop in Omaha, Nebraska.

Our final approach—01 March at approximately 2200 hours—continues in the next chapter.

Don't walk behind me; I may not lead.
Don't walk in front of me;
I may not follow.
Just walk beside me and be my friend.

Albert Camus

7-bravo
Crash

Long ago, on the first of March, 1970,[40] around 2200 hours, I was flying my boss Glenn Schmidt, his wife Carol and my neighbor—a strikingly attractive stewardess named Ann Hudson—back to Chicago from Vail, Colorado, where we had been skiing with a client. Three of us were laughing and having a marvelous time; Carol Schmidt kind of flowed with us, as she was considerably sterner than the rest of us and clearly never approved of my outrageous pursuit of the good life. Our plane, N7856J, was a new Piper Arrow. Per the route that we were following, we were scheduled to stop in Omaha to refuel and then proceed to Chicago's Palwaukee Airport.[41] Denver was obscured by fog and snow when we made our departure, and the bad weather continued to close in around us. With each check of the weather on the airplane radio, it was obvious that the threat was getting closer and closer. With about 40 minutes of fuel in reserve, my plane approached Omaha for its scheduled refueling stop. The weather was rapidly deteriorating, and with a cloud ceiling of 400 feet and only one mile of visibility, we

---

[40] One March is the Natal Day of three awesome Leathernecks – Bob Brent, Jim Gallaway and Sam Badiner.
[41] now Chicago Executive Airport

117

began an instrument approach at IRS Runway 31.

Approximately six miles from the threshold of the runway, we crossed the outer marker. This is where life became riveting. As we approached Omaha's Eppley Airfield, the plane's altimeter was telling me that the plane was 400 feet in the air, but in fact, we were at ground level. We were somewhere between the outer and middle marker of the runway—the point that would later be known as the site of the crash.

The runway is situated on the banks of the Missouri River, and the entire approach happens over the state of Iowa—to be exact, Council Bluffs, Iowa. In late February, the local farmers had just plowed all the fields, leaving soft, straight furrows of dirt in preparation for spring planting. We made good use of them when the plane's left engine dislodged itself completely; the landing gear was sheared away from the plane, and we were jettisoned like empty suitcases. That landing was the equivalent of Disneyland's e-ride,[42] but the

---

[42] Years ago when they passed out coupons at Disneyland, the "e-ride" was always the scariest and most adventure-filled ride. By comparison, the "a-ride" was the merry-go-round.

passengers probably enjoyed it more than the pilot who was busy turning off electronics and cutting off the fuel lines as the Piper Arrow came to rest in that farmer's field, just a few yards from the Missouri River and a couple of clicks[43] away from the end of Runway 31.

The time to thank the Almighty for helping us survive the crash would come later—when we were certain paramedics wouldn't be identifying us from our dental records and farmers from miles around wouldn't be talking about the day those poor bastards went up in a fireball that looked like it could have blown them to Mars. When it seemed like there would be no explosion, we returned and cleared our luggage from the aircraft. Without climbing back into the airplane, I pulled out the radio mike, flipped on the master switch, and called Eppley Field.

"Eppley Tower this is N7458J. It appears that some-where between the outer and middle marker, we have had an emergency landing, and we need transportation." There  was a l-o-n-g silence! The air tower returned, "Would you please repeat that?" Police were immediately dispatched to find us. Their search didn't last long, as we had turned on the plane's red beacon. Quite an entourage appeared to escort us to a motel: a cadre of cops,

---

[43] One click equals 1000 meters.

who unfortunately were accompanied by reporters, and the farmer who owned the field. After a short night of nervous sleeping in the motel's only vacant room, we took a United Airlines flight back to O'Hare.

Under zero-zero conditions, half of the Omaha airport closed shortly after our crash. Years later, when Major Tom Prentice was based at Stratcom in Omaha, we returned to the scene of the crime, determined to find a cause for the accident. Our quest turned up a front-page newspaper article featuring the farmer. His grandfather, still living at the time, talked with us and remembered very clearly the events of that infamous March evening.

There is a tragedy to this story: Carol Schmidt never flew with me again! The FAA's investigation cleared me, but they required me to make three instrument approaches of the same type as a refresher and life punch-down.

Glenn Schmidt, now one of my closest friends and business partners, stuck with me, and we enjoyed a five-year partnership with University Computing Company. All of this happened while we were in our twenties. During that decade, the two of us had the most dramatic rise to success that any two young men could ever expect. If there has to be a moral to the story, this one is as good as any: "The people who are with you when you're flying high learn what you're made of if there's a crash."

Volume III

IRISHMAN

*Who cares how much effort I put in
if it doesn't produce any results?*

Rudy

(from the movie "Rudy")

"Notre Dame Victory March"

Rally sons of Notre Dame
Sing her glory and sound her fame
Raise her Gold and Blue
And cheer with voices true:
Rah, rah, for Notre Dame
We will fight in every game,
Strong of heart and true to her name
We will ne'er forget her
And will cheer her ever
Loyal to Notre Dame.

Cheer, cheer for Old Notre Dame,
Wake up the echoes cheering her name,
Send a volley cheer on high,
Shake down the thunder from the sky!
What though the odds be great or small,
Old Notre Dame will win over all,
While her loyal sons are marching
Onward to victory!

Notre Dame graduates
John F. Shea (words) and Michael J. Shea (music)[44]

---

[44] The piano the Sheas used to compose the song, copyrighted in 1928 and now used by more than 500 schools, remains at the Sorin House on the Notre Dame campus: no wonder Notre Dame never loses!
http://www.youtube.com/watch?v=o_NxSTX0jkc&feature=related
(Search YouTube.com for "Notre Dame Victory March." The video referenced was uploaded by YourFunStop, February 7, 2007.)

*Show me a good and gracious loser,
and I'll show you a failure.*

Knute Rockne

Notre Dame

Chapter 8 is dedicated to Major John Flaherty, a mustang with the true heart of a Marine whose rootin' tootin', rompin' stompin' sons, "Killer and Crash," continue to be the standard bearers for all Irish Leathernecks.

8
Win One For The Gipper:
A Testimony to the Fact that Notre Dame Never Loses

There have been moments throughout history when people of little faith have challenged this assertion, and there will continue to be such moments and such people. In 1971, when my work was based in Houston, and I commuted to a New Orleans office, my stay would extend through Saturday on many occasions. This was a tribute to the culinary delights of New Orleans.

After a year and a half of commuting to Louisiana, my time with that company came to a close; and I was in the process of concluding my underground gourmet experience, having tried almost every four, three, and most—if not all—of the two-star restaurants in town. In my opinion, food is to New Orleans like gambling is to Las Vegas, inherent to the culture and part of the city's backbone.

On one of those weekend culinary excursions, a lady friend named Joy accompanied me. She, like most, was not quite into the culture of the fighting Irish. Since it was a "Notre Dame Saturday," my gear included a portable radio about the size of a cigar box. We went to a two-star restaurant that served the most extraordinary poor-boy sandwiches, purchased these "two-star gourmet" delights, and "went" to the Notre Dame/Purdue game. Our actual location was sunny Jackson Square in New Orleans.

The game opened with Purdue scoring a rather quick touchdown that established a seven-point lead early in the first quarter. Even with heavy rains that turned the field to mud, the game continued and became a virtually scoreless quagmire. At the beginning of the fourth quarter, the score was still Boilermakers, seven points and the Fighting Irish—zero. At that point, the radio quit working. Even yanking the batteries out and putting them back in didn't help. It was obvious to me that sooner or later, Notre Dame would pull the game out without my support from Jackson Square. There wasn't much else to do but suggest to Joy that we walk a few blocks to Pat O'Brien's tavern to introduce her to a famous little drink called the "Hurricane."

As we sat down with our Hurricanes in Jackson Square, my spirits were low because I wanted to know the result of the game. *Exactly how would Notre Dame pull it out?* My radio was sitting on the counter. It had no power, but it was tuned to the right station. Attempting to comfort me, Joy remarked, "Patrick, try not to worry about the game. Even Notre Dame can't win them all." There was only one sane response to such a statement. "You've got to be out of your mind. Notre Dame does win them all! At that moment, Jim Nappo and his son, Jimmy, walked up. As I began to mess with the dials again, a little leather snap on the bottom of the radio came to my attention for the first time. It popped open to reveal an electrical cord that I immediately pulled out. What we needed was an outlet, and our decrepit French Quarter surroundings produced one for us. It was somewhat corroded, but perhaps useable. Walking over to the outlet with radio in hand, I repeated to my friend, "Believe me, Notre Dame never loses." With that came the ceremonial plugging of the cord into the outlet. At that exact moment, the volume came on, and the announcer boomed, "Notre Dame has just scored!" As it turned out, Purdue was making a punt deep into their own end zone, but Notre Dame blocked it. By falling on the ball, Notre Dame gained six points. The score was now seven to six, in favor of the Boilermakers.

The announcer called out, "Notre Dame has elected to go for two." Everyone was commenting about the rain and mud and how the conditions were extremely hazardous. Notre Dame went back, passed, and scored two.

Now, the score was eight to seven in favor of the Fighting Irish . . . and the clock ran out.

I looked at everybody and said, "See, Notre Dame never loses!!!!"

In January 1974, after a rather outstanding season, Notre Dame earned a spot in the Cotton Bowl against the University of Houston.[45] To celebrate the season, my new San Francisco friends agreed to join me at my home on the corner of 29th and Lincoln Way.[46] Bud Swannack and a half dozen other friends came for the game and what was to be Joe Montana's last day in a Notre Dame uniform.

Joe's career at Notre Dame was quite checkered, and he was benched many times. He had been married and divorced and basically did not display the priest-like behavior that Notre Dame administrators consider to be appropriate for Notre Dame. However, toward the end of his last two years at Notre Dame, he set records for last-minute saves. On a side note, Joe Montana's saves, both in college and in professional football, have been compiled in a book—that's how legendary they are.

With the usual holiday bowl atmosphere pervading my home, everyone was watching the game, expecting Notre Dame to win. In Dallas, where the Cotton Bowl is played, the temperature was far below zero, and the score was tied seven to seven. Icicles were dangling from the telephone lines, and the Goodyear Blimp was showing what extraordinarily unusual weather Texas was having. During the middle of the first quarter when Notre Dame was winning

---

[45] Not to be confused with the Cotton Bowl in 1971 when Notre Dame stopped the University of Texas's 33-game running streak with a stunning defeat on New Year's Day
[46] I had moved to San Francisco a year or two earlier; my home was an old, Edwardian-style, four-story house. If you drive by the corner of 29th and Lincoln Way today (as I often encourage people to do), you can still see the Irish Foundation's plaque.

7-0, Joe Montana developed some type of reverse body temperature condition, and his body temperature dropped way below 98 degrees. The announcer said he would be out for the duration of the game. This report, of course, improved the morale and the efforts of Notre Dame's opponent far more than it helped the Fighting Irish.

In the fourth quarter, Notre Dame was losing 34-7, and things looked pretty grim. When I stepped into the kitchen to get something to eat, one of the guys, Pax Bell, turned the channel to the Rose Bowl game between Southern Cal and another Big Ten team. Returning to the living room, I realized my friends had switched the channel from the Notre Dame game. Pax defended his decision. "Well, that game is over. It clearly is *not* a Notre Dame day, so I thought we could watch a game that had more excitement." Of course, Pax's action upset me greatly. Rapidly spinning the TV dial back to the game, I glared at Pax and everyone else in the room and said, "Let me make this perfectly clear: Notre Dame never loses. Now watch!"

At the same time, the phone in my study rang; it was a character from my office named Tom White, who had, over the years, lost a series of bets on Notre Dame to me. In fact, he never won a bet, no matter how generous a point spread he was given. That day, Tom remarked, "Aren't you glad we didn't bet on Notre Dame this week?" When I replied, "Tom, I'm still willing to bet on Notre Dame," he was incredulous. "You mean on the flat, even though they're losing by multiple touchdowns?" My response was the standard, "Yes, you have your bet." (It was a standard $29 bet . . . another story.)

We returned to watching the game when the cameras panned to the sidelines, where Joe Montana was talking to the coach. He had come back from the locker room, saying that he felt a little bit better, and he'd like to try to get back in the game. Notre Dame had possession of the ball. The team went out, and we could sense the huddled team reenergize as Joe Montana replaced his back-up quarterback. The Notre Dame players' adrenaline was rising to the challenge before them.

Montana came into the huddle; they drove for a touchdown and went for two points. The defense squad got up and won immediate custody of the ball. Montana came back in and scored another touchdown and another two points. Finally, we were down to the final two minutes of the game. Notre Dame was driving down the field with the ball and fumbled. Their defense came back in and retrieved the ball for Montana with only a minute left. He immediately drove down the field to the five-yard line. With two seconds left on the clock, the score was 34-28. Joe Montana—the last time he would ever take a hike with the ball in a Notre Dame uniform . . . grabbed the ball, ran back to the left, then far to the right, and threw the ball slightly out of bounds (about three feet off the deck), and Notre Dame's wide receiver caught the ball, with both feet in bounds. This maneuver tied the score 34-34. Notre Dame went back for a kick; a penalty was called, so they had to kick it again a little farther back. Notre Dame scored the last point, breaking the tie, and the game was over. With a score of 35-34, Notre Dame won.

This story proves, once again, the Fighting Irish never lose! Those who don't believe that should at least be wary of betting against them.

A man without honor is nothing.

Winston Churchill

"Notre Dame, Our Mother"

Notre Dame, our Mother

Tender, strong and true

Proudly in the heavens

Gleam thy gold and blue

Glory's mantle cloaks thee

Golden is thy fame

And our hearts forever

Praise thee Notre Dame

And our hearts forever

Love thee Notre Dame!

Music by Joseph Casasanta, a 1923 graduate;
words by the Reverend Charles O'Donnell, C.S.C.,
president of the university at the time of composition[47]

---

[47] The Reverend O'Donnell wrote the lyrics in honor of the university's patroness, Mary, the mother of Jesus.

Patrick, you can be part of the problem,
or you can be part of the solution;
and remember, Patrick,
being respected is more important
than being popular.

Laura Mabel Todd

29 July 1969

Mount Pleasant, Iowa

9-alfa
Clearly, Not Priestly Material

I magine . . . stepping outside of Quigley Seminary and walking down Magnificent Mile in Chicago with one refrain echoing over and over: *How am I going to tell my grandmother that I am no longer going to be a Catholic priest?*

Earlier that day, Monsignor Martin Howard had called me into his impressive office in this 100-year-old Gothic building in the heart of Chicago's Magnificent Mile.[48] This visit to the monsignor's office came at the end of my second year at the legendary school for priests. Monsignor Howard told me, "We don't feel that you have the vocation, and we are not going to invite you back for your third year."

Walking down Michigan Avenue, my prevalent thought was to throw myself into the Chicago River. However, the eight-foot plunge into oily water would be more uncomfortable than deadly; The confrontation with my grandmother would still have to take place, but more dripping and shivering would be involved.

Why did this happen? Rolling down the steps of the Quigley Annex Building in a fight with another student during my second year at

---

[48] Quigley Seminary is located at the edge of the nightclub district.

the seminary probably did not help my discipline record. Also, the enunciation of classical Greek (which was later dropped from the curriculum) did not further my aspirations. The stroke that probably ended my seminary career was my being observed dancing and consorting with some nightclub girls from a nearby neighborhood on the sidewalk near the seminary. In all likelihood, my future celibacy may have been considered a high-risk proposition for the Vatican.

For at least 10 years, shame precluded me from telling anyone about my experiences at seminary. My education was completed at St. Patrick High School, Loyola University and Notre Dame—and my non-priestly life has been more than satisfying. Now, it is okay to speak to attractive women. Eventually, I started sharing the story of my expulsion; now I find it, as do most of my friends, to be a good story with a little bit of humor.

Sadly, the Church has lost touch. They used to take in 500 boys and only about 30 would become ordained 12 years later. In those days, it was competitive. Now, they are having trouble attracting anyone to the priesthood. My friend, Dickie Moore, and I had to pass competitive exams in order to get into Quigley Seminary. Today, they will take anybody, and the seminary is in the process of closing. There is something to be said for 2,000 years of the Catholic Church having standards and living by them in a rock-hard fashion.

If I were the Pope—which is unlikely to happen—women would

be encouraged to become priests and all priests would be allowed to marry. Birth control would be acceptable, as well as a few other practices that would make life in the church a little more palatable. Most modern Catholics have their own version of Catholicism. It still is a pretty good club and mine for life.

In closing, it is possible for laymen and non-priests to become Pope—yet my name is unlikely to be on the College of Cardinals roster the next time they go into the conclave to make a selection. What do you think? Does "Pope Patrick the First" have a nice ring to it? And most importantly, would the Pope be allowed to play polo?

It isn't necessary to see a good tackle.
You can hear it.

Knute Rockne

Notre Dame

Chapter 9-bravo is dedicated to Jim Stepanek of Chicago fame, the best damn friend an incorrigible ever had. "Kimo" too has never seen the Cubs lose a game. God Bless you and June.

9-bravo
Take Me Out To The Ballgame

From 2004 until 2007, my passion for the military and entrepreneurship focused on an exciting enterprise—the expeditionary operation at Pearl Harbor. Due to circumstances well documented, my business venture at Pearl Harbor had to close, but the result was a job well done by everyone involved, particularly Eddie Sherman and Marvin Silverman. This worthy endeavor sent me into a sudden state of working seven days a week, rarely traveling, and not having significant business interests in the island of Oahu. Enter my lifelong friend, Dickie Moore. Since the sixth grade, Dick has been a dear friend to me.

In our lives, we identify many people as "friends." The truth is that we are lucky if we have two, three or four really good friends. Most people we meet should just be called "acquaintances." It's odd that some people—after two or three telephone conversations or a couple of meetings—call me their friend. Clearly, they could not consider me a friend in the truest sense of the word. However, Dick Moore is just that—a true friend and a priceless treasure. He was right there with me in grammar school, and he followed me through our experiences in Catholic seminary, the Marine Corps and two corporations. They say that imitation is the sincerest form of flattery, but Dick's "following" was truly a form of leadership that resulted in his validating my life. From my view, he had every admirable quality that I should have had.

In 2007, Dickie participated in the Chicago Cubs Fantasy Baseball Camp in Mesa, Arizona, and had a great time while making some extraordinary memories.[49] At fantasy baseball camp, you play with the real sports stars and have access to the locker rooms and uniforms; it's like being a new member of the team. Dickie's trip to camp was a grand present from his wife Patti. Unfortunately, he didn't tell me about the fantasy baseball camp until after he returned. Having played baseball with Dickie Moore in grammar school and high school, I considered myself a fairly good ballplayer and wanted to have a go at my old second base position . . . at the Chicago Cubs Fantasy Baseball Camp.

Many years had elapsed since my last ballgame, so I decided to enlist a little help. Coach Kui Kahooilihala at Roosevelt High School in Honolulu understood my challenge, and he and his baseball team adopted me. For about two months in late 2007, I went to every batting cage on the island, chased fly balls, and fielded copious grounders batted to me by Kahooilihala, one great coach.

After arriving in Arizona and checking in at the team hotel for my stay, I showed up early for the first morning of fantasy baseball camp,

---

[49] Mesa is located near Phoenix.

walked into the locker room, and saw a real Chicago Cubs uniform, just for me. In fact, they gave me two uniforms—one for traveling and one for home games. Both uniforms sported the number 29 and the name Brent monogrammed above the number. In about two and a half milliseconds, I whipped out my camera and was in Chicago Cubs heaven.

We had two practice games a day and ate lunch in the locker rooms with hall-of-famers like Billy William and Ernie Banks, plus other Chicago Cubs stars and staff. Chicago Cubs coaches and staff trained us on four perfectly manicured diamonds. Joe Pepitone conducted our first team meeting, which was just fine by me.

Why was it fine? Clearly, all of this was a travesty that ended in justice. Each day after practice, I returned to my hotel and climbed into an oversized hot tub occupied by two or three other players and a large-sized, middle-aged guy. We assessed each other, after which he responded obliquely to my questions about how his life was going and how his team was doing, and life rolled on.

It turned out that my hot tub mate was one of the head Chicago Cubs coaches, who also had been a former Cubs player and New York Yankees pitcher. Furthermore, my conversations with him had been considered disrespectful, and my punishment was to be a $20 fine. Just as the fine was being levied, I walked into the room and immediately protested it. Standing in front of 65 or 70 Fantasy Camp attendees, I stated my case. "This fine is totally unfair and in fact it should be reversed and it should be paid by the gentlemen who imposed it upon me." My jury smiled and asked me why. "Because he impersonated a Fantasy Camp camper. He truly was out of condition in that hot tub and did not look like the great athlete. Plus, although he played seven years with the New York Yankees (I had done my homework before I got there), he was with the Cubs for only one year. I have that from good knowledge. My friend, Dickie Moore, and I have spent more time standing in the hot dog line at Wrigley Field than he spent playing with the Cubs. Therefore, given the fact that he impersonated an out-of-shape, middle-aged camper and the fact that he was not a Cub in the true spirit of the word, the fine should be reversed." Obviously, my life's calling is not law; the jury of campers doubled my fine.

We had a grand week. Whenever we had a break, I went to the batting cage. Getting ahead of the game at Fantasy Camp is very easy. Most of the campers were middle-aged gentlemen from the Midwest, and they were not in great shape. Although they probably were far better athletes in their younger years, my daily "P.T." over the years had given me quite an edge; and that was my program. A dedicated exercise regimen pays off when you do something like Fantasy Camp.

On the final day of camp, my team, my favorite pal, Cole Dooley, a farmer from central Illinois, and I played against an all-star Chicago Cub team at the stadium in Mesa in front of 20,000 people. By the seventh inning, the bases were loaded, and the pitcher turned out to be my hot tub nemesis, former New York Yankees great, Steve "Rainbow" Trout! He turned to his teammates, all famous Chicago Cubs baseball players, and said, "This is the guy from the hot tub—the one who was fined." They all kind of smiled. After stepping out of the batter's box, and with a bow to the infield and a bow to the audience (all captured on camera, of course), I returned to the batter's box to wait for my pitch. It came high and fast and whizzed just behind my head, causing me to duck. Being reasonably certain that this pitch was deliberate gave me the shakes for a moment, so I stepped out of the batter's box again to collect myself. "Rainbow" obviously wanted to make a point. His next pitch to me was a strike. The following pitch flew right down the middle at medium speed and was clearly a gift. That hit to deep left center field cleared most of the bases and gave me one great and unforgettable Chicago Cub moment. After making his point, perhaps "Rainbow" had decided to be kind.

After doing so well at Chicago Cubs Fantasy Camp (Irish grin), it was time for me to pursue a football career—and where else but with the Fighting Irish of Notre Dame? When my daughter was filling out the application forms for Notre Dame's MBA program, she found the Web site for Notre Dame's Fantasy Camp, which had been open for a few years already; if I had known about it then, I would have signed up to attend the first year! The Chicago Cubs Camp was somewhat expensive, and the thought crossed my mind that perhaps it was too much money for the experience. The Notre Dame Camp was 40 or 50 percent more costly, but that cost never bothered me. Certainly, playing football at Notre Dame would be worth the fee. In fact, I called and sent in my money without reading all of the information on the website. My intention was to be a part of the June 2008 Fantasy Camp on the Notre Dame campus. That's what mattered.

My intention and desire presented a certain dilemma—how to be a football player when one has never played football. To remedy my problem, I returned to Coach Kui at Roosevelt High School; at the time, his son was Roosevelt's star quarterback. For two months, they took me out to Ala Moana Beach Park and other locations around the high school where they trained me to throw a football and do typical football camp exercises. Each two-hour training session provided me with four hours worth of sweat. Good physical training was another step toward Notre Dame.

During my travels leading up to June, I would stop at a local Target or Kmart, buy a $10 football, and play catch with anybody who would hang out with me. Oddly enough (or perhaps not), every guy in the world wants to play catch, so carrying footballs around became quite a hobby of mine. Some of the impromptu players kept the footballs, which had "on my way to Notre Dame" scrawled on them with a magic marker.

Just a few days before traveling to Indiana, I was at Quantico, doing the annual run-amok with Rick Nealis, the race director of the Marine Corps Marathon. Our downtime was another opportunity to play football with anyone who would throw the ball back to me. When the commandant's long-time attorney, Peter Murphy, and I were scheduled to have lunch in Washington, D.C., my football came with me—and there, on a sidewalk in Chinatown, were more willing receivers. For about three months, I was in my own fantasy camp, getting ready for Notre Dame!

In June, I arrived in Indiana for Notre Dame's Fantasy Football Camp a couple of days early and stayed at Dick Moore's home. Upon check-in at Notre Dame, the staff assigned one of the senior Fantasy Campers (60 percent are people who return) to me, and we took a football out and tossed it for a while.

Finally, the first day of Fantasy Camp arrived. We received all of our equipment and home and away game uniforms in the Fighting Irish blue and gold— our blessed Virgin's colors. Once again, mine came with the lucky number 29. Every morning, we went out for physical fitness training and various types of  football training. Even though I weighed in as the lightest member of our entire 60-man football squad, I declared myself one of the four quarterback candidates.

On the Friday night before our big game, NBC came out for an interview.[50] The NBC journalist was not too interested in the camp, and to add distaste to disinterest—he wasn't an advocate of Notre Dame. His attitude provoked me and generated a fun interview that NBC showed repeatedly. Game-day Saturday dawned, and all of us— Fantasy Campers, the Notre Dame trainers, the real Notre Dame coaches, and Notre Dame's head coach, Charlie Weiss—assembled in the locker room from which we had been training every day that week. We left the locker room and headed toward the tunnel of cheering fans, with the PA system blaring the Notre Dame Fight Song in the famous Notre Dame Stadium—the house that Knute Rockne built. We ran through the tunnel and on to the firing zone with a handful of other gentlemen who knew Notre Dame tradition and knelt to say a Hail Mary. Earlier in the locker room, in addition to keeping certain time-honored Notre Dame pre-football game traditions, we had offered, "Our Lady of Victory, pray for us." As we went down the staircase to the tunnel, I pounded the sign, "Play Like a Champion Today," created by Lou Holtz many years ago.

We had a great game, with as many trappings as Notre Dame could possibly furnish. Approximately 400-500 people were in the audience; some of those were a group of Marine Reservists and Marines who ran the Notre Dame ROTC program, plus my good

---

[50] The interview is available on YouTube.

friend Dickie Moore, and a few other friends as well. My turn at quarterback was everything one might imagine!

During the whole of the game, only one touchdown was scored. Two Notre Dame teams were playing—the gold team and the blue team. The blue team won 6-0, and my team was gold. Neither team had very good kickers, but at the end of the game, we all mustered up. All of us assembled and sang the Notre Dame alma mater, "Tender, Strong, and True," possibly one of the greatest songs in the world. After the game, we had a banquet where we each were awarded a genuine Notre Dame helmet. Mine is proudly displayed in my home in Hawaii. A Superbowl trophy wouldn't have felt like more of a prize that day.

A week later, my name was on the list for the next camp session. Due to some post-graduate coursework taken at Notre Dame, courtesy of Father Joyce when I was working on a Univac 1107 contract many years ago, I consider myself a quasi alumnus. Unlike the title character from the movie "Rudy" and a few others, I must have lacked courage and fortitude because I did not do my undergraduate work at Notre Dame, although it was an option. As a St. Patrick High School student, I was accepted at Notre Dame; but the cost was five times what it was to attend a Catholic college in Chicago, so passing seemed to be the right thing to do. Even though I was only 17 when that decision was made, I clearly lacked whatever Rudy and others had that they used to make Notre Dame work for them. It's one of those forks in the road that one reflects on for a long time.

Thanks to the Fantasy Camp and other experiences, such as giving a lecture on journalism and Marine Corps history there in the fall of 2008, Notre Dame is a part of my fabric and always will be.

GOD BLESS THE IRISH!

Hisako with Notre Dame football player and
2012 Heisman Trophy Runner-up, Manti Te'o

"My Beliefs"

I believe in the immortal soul, sunrises, Chicago pizza, European dark chocolate, the Chicago Cubs, good red wine, Hawaiian sunsets and the small of a women's back.

I believe Lee Harvey Oswald acted alone (and was an accurate sharp shooter).

I believe we need a constitutional amendment against overpaid baseball players and trashy soda machines.

I believe in red-headed women, John Wayne, Hula dancers, geishas and femininity.

I believe in Leathernecks, the sweet spot, Victoria's Secret, Buddha and the Pope.

I believe in fast horses, long ocean swims, penalty one polo shots, thunderstorms, and our flag . . . and that Notre Dame never loses!

I believe in opening your presents on Christmas morning not Christmas Eve.

I believe in "whites" only in tennis and polo.

And . . . I believe in long, deep, soft kisses that last two days.

Amen

A Domer pal from Paris named Bill suggested a picture section so the USC football team readers can also revel in this Irish legacy ...

With then Major Tom Prentice, USMC (0302 TSOCP)   Marine Rifleman in Iraq

Reporter P.T. Brent in Djibouti / Horn of Africa post a violent storm with French Foreign Legion, spring 2004

Then Marine Lt. Josh Bates on run up to Bagdad in 2003

Recovering from wounds sustained in Husaybah, Iraq, then Staff Sergeant Adam Walker is pictured here.

7 December 1942
Pearl Harbor Marine Memorial; seventy-three Marines are still entombed.

In Kandahar with U.S. Army Infantry

Wake Island 2010 with Wayne White the Marine vet in charge

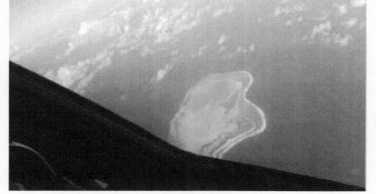

Wake Island from USAF C17

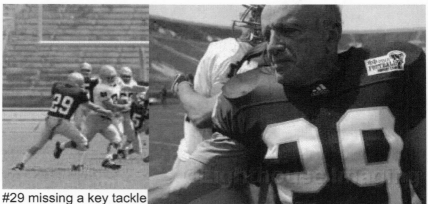

#29 missing a key tackle
on N.D. player "Country"   Coin toss by team captains

Scarlett at Will Rogers polo with Mickey Brittan

Just cleared the bases; high 5 with Cole Dooley, 23, Illinois farmer

Laura Brent is pictured with her husband, Lieutenant Benjamin Walker, number one TBS graduate, at the home of the Commandant.

Ronald Regan, a dedicated horseman, receiving a mallet

P.T. and Laura
25 December 2010,
run/swim Hawaii

Robert Brent, 1937 China Marine

Uncle Donald Reiter, WWI Leatherneck

Volume IV

CORRESPONDENT

Dedicated to Ernie Pyle, a truly gifted war correspondent, who vis a vis Eddie Sherman, inspired this third-rate journalist to strive a little harder and make his stories come alive.

OOO-RRAH, Ernie Pyle.

Ernest Taylor Pyle (1900-1945) was an American journalist and war correspondent whose writing was syndicated in hundreds of newspapers. He reported on World War II from North Africa, Europe and the South Pacific. He was killed by Japanese gunfire during the U.S. invasion of Okinawa. He wrote "Here Is Your War" (1943) and "Brave Men" (1944), and won the Pulitzer Prize in 1944 for his stories about "the ordinary men" fighting WWII.

All that is necessary
for the triumph of evil
is for good men to do nothing.

Edmund Burke, 18th century Irishman

Chapter 10-alfa is dedicated to Colonel John Bates,

one hell of a gyrene.

10-alfa
How To Be A Combat Journalist With Zero Experience

During the first Gulf War, when my friend, John Bates, and his battalion invaded and rescued the country of Kuwait, this Marine felt left out of the action. It didn't seem right to sit at home and watch it on television.

When Colonel Bates shipped off for the second Gulf War in 2003, I told him that yet again I felt out of it. John commented to me, "Well, you know, you've done a lot of work on your magazine *Polo Gazette* and various other articles, and the Pentagon is embedding hundreds of journalists in various combat units. Why don't you come over as a journalist?"

With only a few weeks left before the war kicked off, trying to go through the proper channels to get things done was daunting and frustrating; things weren't happening! Finally, I received assurances that a visa would be waiting for me upon my arrival in Kuwait City.[51] To be on the safe side, I also contacted the president of Bradford-Adams and Company, a corporation of which I was the majority shareholder, and instructed the president to have someone create a

---

[51] Of course, said visa did not materialize when I landed in Kuwait City.

journalist's credential for me. After all, the company was a publishing firm. He replied that credentials were not their forte and that they usually did not do that sort of thing. How else could I respond except, "Tom, you know I'm going to have that credential, and it is going to be a really handsome one that will be waiting for me when I arrive at the Gulf Hotel in Kuwait City—or the *new* president of Bradford-Adams will have an identification card for me." Tom, being the very astute man that he is, replied, "Just how do you want that to look, and where do we send it?"

Upon my arrival, my first journalist's credential was there, although my visa had not arrived, which delayed me at the Kuwait City airport for about an hour and a half. That gave me just enough time to purchase some really great lunches and dinners for airport staff and immigration officials. Later, I met the minister of information for the country of Kuwait and learned about the incredibly horrific things that Saddam Hussein and his sons had done to people during their reign. I have never written down or discussed the things they did to their own citizens. The war may have been a mistake; clearly we were not prepared to occupy the country. Regardless of one's opinions on that, everyone can rest assured that sending Saddam and his sons directly to hell was a worthwhile project.

Within a few days of my arrival, I was armed with letters of introduction to several key people and credentials from the Minister of Kuwait, the United States Navy, the United States Army, and—of course—our Marines. My Irishman's luck found me embedded with General Conway (who later became our Commandant) with 1MEF—the Marine expeditionary force, and two days after St. Patrick's Day, the battle was launched. After spending 10 additional days in the area to write stories for the "Hawaii Reporter" and capturing a front-page spot on 14 consecutive issues of the "Honolulu Star-Bulletin," I headed for home, thinking the war was over. The most action I saw included a few artillery rounds and some spurious Iraqi missiles that missed their targets by a mile.

A lesson learned while covering the Iraq and Afghanistan war, to my everlasting happiness, was that the enemy never went to their firing range. Their marksmanship was random and casual, and the odds of their hitting you were pretty slim—very much unlike being shot at by a U.S. Marine who spends more time on the range then any of the other armed service branches.

A year later, General Grayson and General McAbee were telling people that my stories were the most positive press the Marine Corps had received in a long while. Unlike the first trip, there would be no hassles getting back over there; they were clambering to give me press credentials and to furnish transportation to exotic climes such as Afghanistan, Iraq, and later Djibouti, Africa. United Press International (UPI), as well as the Honolulu papers, hired me to do another series of stories. My initial run up to Baghdad had been straightforward and fairly easy to accomplish; the post-war trip was completely contrary and much more difficult. The IEDs[52] were designed more cleverly and more ubiquitously. During my second and third trips, artillery fire was much more random on base, as were rockets and tracers; and of course, getting around the roads became close to impossible at times. Insurgents owned the highways. Three separate convoys in which I was embedded were fired upon as we traveled from Ballad to Fallujah.

An uncomfortable second trip (post-war), included time spent in Afghanistan—mostly in Kandahar, and later, in Iraq within one month. As part of my bargain with the generals, I promised to cover Djibouti, Africa, representing the Marine Corps in a place where no press had been taken since the establishment of Camp Lemoyne in the Horn of Africa near Djibouti City.

After that trip, filthy and worn out, while trying to get a flight home at the airstrip, I found out, via a DSN government phone line, from a voice message left on my home phone in Honolulu, that my

---

[52] IEDs = improvised explosive devices

mother had passed away and that my sister refused to delay the funeral for a day or two so that I could get there. I got on a C-130 headed from Djibouti to Qatar. Arriving in Qatar at about 2100 hours on a night devoid of stars, I went down the ramp and was greeted by a young major I've known since he was two weeks old. Over a couple of beers, we caught up on what he was doing in Qatar and traded some sea stories.

Major Tom Prentice (now Lt. Colonel Tom Prentice) helped me reconcile my incorrigible sister's behavior. It seemed like a good time to take a vacation, and a C-17 bound non-stop from Qatar to Ramstein, Germany, became my transport. In Ramstein, I spent time with wounded Marines and made a few lifelong friends. During my visits with them, it was essential from time to time to walk around the corner for a minute, because my eyes were tearing up.[53] Despite the enormity of their injuries, all of those Marines wanted to heal as quickly as they could so that they could rejoin their units and keep their jobs. There wasn't an ounce of false bravado in the group. They were just great Americans wanting to do their jobs. God, was I proud of them!

After my visit to Ramstein and some vacation time in Italy, I headed home and announced to the Marine Corps and my various supporters that my combat journalism career was over. There were just too many close calls.

---

[53] Marines, of course, do not cry.

Six months later, I was attending a reception on an aircraft with several Navy admirals, Marine generals, and my daughter. One of the generals announced that he had the general's G4[54] and would be shoving off for many different locations in Afghanistan, Iraq, and Africa, along with P.T. Brent, who would be traveling with him and his staff and crew. Surprised, I started to say, "Didn't I tell you . . . " but the general interrupted me. "No, we've got this all set up." Everyone was staring at me, which intensified the pressure; I hesitated for a moment and then capitulated. "Include me." It was late August, and there I was, heading back to make connections in Tampa and take off for Africa, Afghanistan, and a place called Firebase Shkin.

Major Jody Lynch, whom I knew from Honolulu, when he worked under Colonel Bates in the 2nd Battalion 3rd Marines, met the general's helicopter at Firebase Shkin. He greeted me with, "Hot shit! Wait 'til I tell Colonel Bates that Mr. Brent is here!" In the spirit of the moment, I replied, "Well, you ought to go to &*^* and get yourself a weapon!" With Major Lynch and Col. Bates around, it seemed like old home week on the Afghanistan/Pakistan border.

Later, during our tour, the general and I made the cover of every Iraqi newspaper. On 11 September, 2004, while we were traveling between al Taqqadum and Fallujah, our convoy of six humvees was ambushed by insurgents on the side of the highway after they misfired

---

[54] known as the Grey Ghost

two IEDs that exploded between the vehicles. The Marines in the 50 caliber positions and the Marines from the windows of the humvees destroyed these men in a few seconds. Once again, marksmanship! It was the first real fire fight several of the people in the convoy had seen. When we pulled into Fallujah, one noticed my patch with 2nd Battalion 24th Marines and asked, "Where'd you get this?" I replied, "That's my old 'blankety-blank' unit." His answer astounded me. "Well, all the Marines in this convoy were from 2nd Battalion 24th Marines Chicago." Needless to say, we still have reunions and chat about that day.

The following day, 12 September, was an historical one. We experienced the change of command between the One I MEF—that is, General Conway turning the One I MEF over to General Solder. During the press conference that announced the change of command, I asked the only positive question. Fortunately, after everything was over, we did not drive back to the airfield at al Taqqadum. We took a helicopter with the two generals to al Taqqadum and flew out of a 130 at Baghram, Afghanistan. We had a nice dinner and took a red eye to Paris where I proceeded to do a couple of stories for "Polo Magazine." After leaving the Marines—especially the ones who were in harm's way—that feeling of being out of place returned. It is quite difficult to settle into being a civilian again. After a day and a half of my return to "normal" life, I chose to forego a weekend of parties and took my rental car to Omaha Beach for a couple of days. After a couple of dozen trips to France, this trip marked my first pilgrimage to Omaha Beach. At the time, it meant a lot to be back with warriors as opposed to people just having a good time.

Thus, my third combat journalism trip ended. In the meantime, I wrote for "Leatherneck" magazine. One of my favorites pieces was about General John Archer Lejeune (Luh Jern) (Luh Jern) (Luh Jern), the history of the man who is considered by many, including myself, to be the world's greatest Leatherneck. There were also stories about Marine One, embassies in Hong Kong, Dublin, and Copenhagen, and a story about the Defense Language Institute in Monterey, California, featuring my friend Corporal Benjamin Walker—now Lieutenant Walker—who had just met his future wife there.

Perhaps the time has come for me to write books about life, sensuality, and things that do not involve incoming artillery fire.

The secret to a good sermon
is to have a good beginning
and a good ending –
and to have the two
as close together as possible.

George Burns

1 April 1944

Chapter 10-bravo is dedicated to Major Christopher Hughes (now Colonel Hughes), the best public affairs office in the United States Marine Corps. (Major Hughes bailed P.T.B. out of the Kuwait airport jail during his first attempt to be a third-rate journalist.)

10-bravo
Atrocities Incredulous

Editor's Note: This story was originally published by the "Hawaii Reporter" in 2004.

One Navy corpsman said he could not understand the coalition forces standard of: "Shock and Awe." He stated that since we were kids, the good guys always gave the other guys a chance to drop their guns and raise their hands. Why . . . why this display of might in Baghdad? All over the world, a minority, albeit vocal group, are creating discord over "Bush's war." Perhaps they have a point. Clearly, in retrospect, the Vietnam protestors were on target with their cry of an unjust war.

In reality, happenstance made them right. They were like today's indignant protestors doing their thing to be fashionable. History has made them righteous . . . and lucky.

This is no Vietnam by any stretch of the imagination. This is the reincarnation of Hitler, Mussolini, Stalin and Hirohito of World War II infamy. The people of Iran have had few sympathies with Saddam removal. They, like the Kuwaiti and his own people, have experienced genocide at his hands. The average of the last two polls taken by the "Arab News" and the "Kuwaiti Times" state that 89.6 percent of the people support the war as long as Saddam is removed for good.

Perhaps they have a different perspective than these protestors.

Last night, after returning to "K.C.," Kuwait City's Ministry of Information (Suchrain Sarah Al-Deyyain) invited this scribe to visit the recently created museum of Iraqi atrocities. It seems to maintain a low profile. Perhaps, because the media hesitates or will not report scenes that are beyond human comprehension. This tragic recreation should have been done 10 to 12 years ago. It should be redone by Hollywood and shared with the world. The Holocaust museum in Washington, D.C., is comparable. Remarkably, the Kuwaitis and the Israelis have a common cause: the eradication of an evil regime.

If each and every protestor could take one hour to walk through these passageways filled with photographic, video and graphic displays of unimaginable horror, they would do a 180-degree switch of their position. Once they had recovered from the tears, disgust and stomach-churning atrocities, this vile human being and the vermin he breeds would not have the support of a single good person.

The only question left would be when and how an Iraqi tribunal will send Saddam's butt straight to a well-deserved hell.

P.T. Brent O U T

P.T. Brent is a Hawaii business man and U.S. Marine infantry veteran. He has been embedded with the Marines in Iraq and other conflict areas for the past 60 days.

'Til the stars grow old
'Til the sun grows cold
'Til the leaves of the Judgment Book unfold,
May there be a Corps of Marines, and
may they uphold the legacy.

Major Ralph Stoney Bates, USMC (Ret.)

11
Fallujah's Rocky Road

Editor's note: this article was written for UPI on Sept. 11, 2004

Yyyyeeeooww bang![55]

On the road to Fallujah

An improvised explosive device explodes between the fifth and sixth Marine Humvees, narrowly missing that of Gen. Jerry McAbee. The remaining vehicles in our convoy accelerate through a cloud of acid smoke. Simultaneously, six AK47 rifles and one light machine gun open fire on the Marine convoy.

Within a fraction of a second, Marines with 50-caliber

---

[55] Borrowed from the style of Ernie Pyle, greatest journalist of WWII; Thanks and Mahalo to editor Eddie Sherman for telling me to "read Pyle"!

machine guns, 40mm heavy machine guns, 7.62mm light machine guns, and M16 rifles respond from all six vehicles.

Their performance is professional and lethal, well-reflecting their training and experience. They unload an accurate and deadly hail of bullets down upon the attackers.

Corp. Gomez's rifle spews out a stream of hot expended cartridges, repeatedly striking my face. Not to worry, this correspondent is busy trying to figure out how to pull his Kevlar helmet down around his knees. When I ask Gomez for his first name, he tells me that it is "Corporal, sir."

Staff Sgt. Paul Zogg, a Marine reservist from Chicago (2nd Battalion, 24th Marine Regiment), Convoy Commander, immediately pivots his lead vehicle into a 180-degree turn and backtracks in support of the last vehicles still under attack. His response is second nature.

Command has automatically switched to Sgt. Jeff McCoy, a reservist from Riverside, California, who orders Gomez to fire off a report to IMEF Headquarters. Meanwhile, Sgt. Arthur Green, a San Diego reservist, is firing his Mark-19 heavy machine gun at the attackers armed with AK47s, the insurgents' weapon of choice. When the situation is under control, the staff sergeant from Chicago returns to the lead position and resumes command.

The other vehicles in the convoy also respond superbly. Even McAbee gets into the action. After we arrived at our destination, Corp. Hammond, another "corporal," comes up and says that McAbee did a great job of passing the ammo belts up to his machine gun position.

Col. John Jackson, chief of staff, says after the firefight, "As I have always said . . . it is better to be fired at and missed," and Col. Phil Yff comments, "I don't recall anybody looking me in the eye." This remark by Yff is in reference to a conversation I'd had with him the day before.

He relates that to reassure his wife during Desert Storm, he would tell her not to worry about the Scuds. "Nothing's going to fall out of the sky and kill me," he would say. "If I'm going to die in the desert, somebody whose willpower is greater than mine has got to look me in the eye and kill me.

"When your number is up, your number is up."

Another senior officer comments on how on Sept. 11, this third anniversary of terrorism's biggest day, there had been no hits within the target-rich United States.

The idea of "Fortress America" is a myth. Right now, we have them on the run, or at least, for today we do. We also have the Iraqi insurgents over here, far away from the American people.

The imminent possibility of death, perhaps alone in a faraway land is daunting. However, these Marines from Camp Pendleton are completing their second tour in Iraq. They live with it[56] 24 hours a day, each and every day.

McCoy, on Gen. Hejlik's security staff, says, "Sure, we average two

---

[56] "It" is the idea of death.

or three mortar rounds a day at Camp Fallujah, but they are not very accurate." He wants to return to his wife and two daughters as well as to his job as a marketing executive with Anheuser-Busch. He is grateful that his company pays his full salary while he is deployed—a patriotic partnership between employer and Marine reservist.

In this land of fatalistic outlook, they say, "No man can guarantee his own fate." However, these Marines at Camp Fallujah are trying.

You think dogs will not be in heaven?
I tell you, they will be there
long before any of us.

Robert Louis Stevenson

A salute to Major Rich Linsday who was CEO of the organization that graduated the 50,00 Devil Pups - 2011, Camp Pendleton; BZ, Ritchie.

12

Send In The Doggone Marines

Editor's note: This story was originally published in the "Star-Bulletin" on Sunday, 18 April 2004

Cchyna, bred by the corps and tattooed Delta-043, is the pride of the Marine Corps' expanding dog tracker and security units. She's an MWD, Marine War Dog. A Belgian Malau born Sept. 12, 1999, Cchyna is trained to go ahead of Marines and sniff out explosives and hidden snipers or terrorists. Perhaps named after the legendary Fourth Marines of Shanghai fame, she is the close working pal of Marine Sgt. Dan Wheeler.

This canine Leatherneck knows her stuff. At Guantanamo, Cchyna was used as

P.T. BRENT PHOTO
Cchyna, a Marine War Dog, takes a break from sniffing for bombs in Fallujah to strike a pretty pose for the camera.

a "mind deterrent" with Afghan detainees. After some time off recently to heal from a broken foot, Cchyna is now with Master Dan in red-hot Fallujah to sniff out IEDs in Iraq.

These dogs are treasured for their loyalty and their price tag. As pups, they cost $2,000; after training they are valued at more than $60,000. When one dies, it is buried with full Marine honors. There is a special war dog cemetery at Camp Lejeune (Luh Jern), N.C., with grave markers recounting the history of the deceased. There lie some 30 dogs that gave life and faithful service to the Marine Corps.

P.T. BRENT PHOTO

Cchyna, a Marine War Dog, eyes a tennis ball in a teasing match with her trainer, Marine Sgt. Dan Wheeler.

The graduates of the new dog tracker program are tracker-oriented and will be assigned to Osama bin Laden's backyard.

Wheeler, a gentleman from Grand Rapids, Michigan,[57] is a soft-

---

[57] Grand Rapids, Michigan, is also the hometown of former President Gerald Ford.

spoken, classic Marine sergeant. He played football and ran track at Rogers High School, class of '97. His mom, Theresa, taught at Rogers Elementary for more than 20 years, and his dad, David, worked at Grand Rapids water treatment facility after a hitch as a Navy Seabee.

After attending Ferris State, Wheeler joined the Marine Corps because his Uncle Gary, a "cool guy," was a Leatherneck. Later, his Uncle Tony suggested K-9 Corps activity, and Wheeler re-enlisted to get the assignment. He is seeking a commission program in the Corps. When asked about the war dissenters, Wheeler replied, "My family has always served. These people know that they are wrong."

Wheeler's elder brother was a Seabee; another brother, a firefighter; and younger brother, Justin, may join the Marine Corps after he graduates from Rogers High this year. His wife, Sara, also comes from a family with a Corps tradition.

The daunting task of rebuilding Iraq is overwhelming in comparison to waging the war. Iraq has the resources and the people to make it the arena of a renaissance of the Muslim world. Let's pray the Iraqis give us a chance to help them.

This is a most auspicious moment to take pride in America and our forces overseas. Do you remember pride in our country? We used to have it by the carload. Forget whether or not you agree with taking on Saddam Hussein; just get yourself a flag and wave it proudly. Let's pray for our distant warriors, and let's bring our young Americans home safely.

The faces of these Leathernecks may seem younger—faces like Sgt. Dan Wheeler's and Capt. Chris Borzi's from Poughquaq, N.Y. (U.S. Naval Academy, 1996). But the packs and the rifles, they weigh as much. The heat, dust, cold, and long night marches are all still there. Yes, the faces may appear younger, but beneath the surface runs the same blood that stained and won battlefields from Tripoli to Iwo Jima, and from Guadalcanal to Iraq.

They are the same outfit. The United States Marine Corps.

*Every leader, and every regime,
and every movement,
and every organization
that steps across the line to terrorism
must be banished from the discourse
of civilized human life.*

Alan Keyes (speech, April 2002)

Chapter 13 is dedicated to Joanne Glennon, whose loyalty, patience and friendship in editing war stories raised this author to almost a journalist. Mahalo nui loa from Hawaii!

13

U.S. Marines Bring Hope to a Poor African Nation

Editor's note: This story was originally published in the "Star-Bulletin" on Sunday, 9 May 2004

Djibouti, Horn of Africa: A Jeep bus careens wildly around a corner and the side mirror whacks the head of a local man; he drops, apparently dead. Djiboutians take little notice. Life is cheap is this lawless land.

Major Tom Prentice, a Marine from Texas, calls Djibouti "the kind of place where you'd expect to see Indiana Jones." This former French colony, contiguous with Ethiopia and Somali, is

PHOTO COURTESY OF M.D. MUNOZ
A woman waits for water provided by Marines, who are in Djibouti to provide flood relief and to fend off al-Qaida.

in a tough neighborhood. According to the Marine Corps commanding officer Col. Bill Callahan, an Irishman from West Hartford, Conn., the primary values are location, location and location.

Djibouti (ja-BOOT-ti) is on the Horn of Africa, at the crossroads of the Red Sea, Yemen, Somalia, Kenya, Ethiopia, and of course, Arabia's rich oil fields. It is slightly smaller than Massachusetts, with a population of 600,000 mostly Muslim Africans. It has virtually a zero economy with little potable water; and the life expectancy for a Djiboutian born today is barely 40 years. This sorrowful statistic is no doubt well-assisted by the AIDS epidemic that scientists believe originated in Africa; sadly, 12 percent of Djiboutians now have HIV. One of the Djiboutians' few recreations is a stimulant called "khat," which they get from chewing the leaves of the catha edulis plant.

Each day at 1300, the Marines see the cargo plane from Ethiopia land with the daily khat sales to be distributed through a legally organized set of vendors. Khat is widely used even in the highest circles of government.

Travel here is at your own risk. The roads have no signage, even at railway crossings. Livestock wander onto the highways. Vehicles, free of safety measures, often seem to be out of control.

Terrorists will thrive in these lands without governance. America had to learn this the hard way. Where we failed to stop Osama bin Laden in Ethiopia and Afghanistan, we now intend to stop al-Qaida from establishing a base on or near the Horn of Africa. Thus enter the Marines, who now have satellite bases on Kenya's coast and in Ethiopia, operated from Djibouti as part of Operation Enduring Freedom. The Marines also provide humanitarian relief, which currently includes re-building whatever structures were destroyed and purifying water tainted by recent flooding in the normally arid region.

Djibouti is a hardship post for the Corps; usually no more than a six-month deployment is required. This small base is reminiscent of the old posts in Latin America, where Marines often represented the only semblance of law and order.

During the Gulf War, Djibouti was the base of operations for French forces, and France still maintains a garrison of the renowned French Foreign Legion. President Omar Gelleh is a strong ruler who favors Djibouti's long-standing relationship with France. He also favors the economic assets that the United States offers his country. The Germans also have some forces in Djibouti. Perhaps France and Germany, too, would have been targets in Djibouti land, had their governments not vetoed the U.S. resolutions at the United Nations.

Djibouti is the third point in the AOR[58] triangle. Our Marine general officers, Lt. Gen. Chip Gregson and Brig. Gen. Jerry McAbee from Oahu have the responsibility for this area, as well as the Iraqi and Afghanistan areas. Meanwhile, our Marines stand guard at a post

---

[58] AOR = area of responsibility

in a critical location in the global war on terrorism. "Be assured," says Col. Callahan, "this will not be a future home for al-Qaida."

People sleep peaceably
in their beds at night
only because rough men stand ready
to do violence on their behalf.

George Orwell

14

Elite French Fighters Join Marines:

The famed French Foreign Legion aids relief work in Africa

Editor's note: This story was originally published in the "Star-Bulletin" on Sunday, 9 May 2004.

PHOTO COURTESY OF M.D. MUNOZ

The U.S. Marines and the French Foreign Legion are working together to bring relief to Djibouti, a normally arid African nation hit hard recently with storms and the ensuing flooding.

Djibouti, Horn of Africa:

"If you turn me down once more, I'll join the French Foreign Legion."

"Au revoir, cherie. It's the French Foreign Legion for me…"

This Frank Sinatra ballad laments going off to join the French Foreign Legion after your girl turns you down. Well, men from 120 countries have done just that, although perhaps not all for that reason. The legendary Legion Etrangère are 7,500 strong. Seventy percent of the enlisted are not French, but 90 percent of the officers are. Lt. Col. Benoit Durieux, graduate of Saint

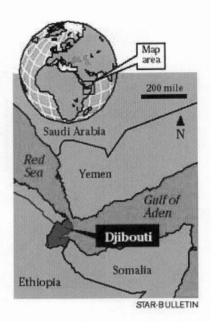

Cyr Academie in Brittany, gave us some of the famed Legion's history.

Only one out of every eight men who try to enlist makes the grade. Many are given new identities for protection. After five years, the term of enlistment, they are eligible for French citizenship. They train four months in Castelnaudary; and of course, one of the subjects teaches all of those men from different countries how to speak French. Clearly not for the faint-hearted, the Legion stands out among elite fighting organizations. It generates more mystery and romance than any other unit worldwide. Legionnaires are part of the French Army but are known by their distinctive Seven Flame Grenade insignia.

Legion regulations would raise the eyes even of our disciplined Marines:

Legionnaires using assumed identities are not allowed to have bank accounts.

A Legionnaire cannot own a motor vehicle or marry until meeting several conditions, including being enlisted at least five years and using his own identity.

They must live in barracks and are not permitted to wear civilian clothes during the first five years.

Should they return late from liberty, they will receive 10 days in prison.

They must not leave France until they have been in the Legion for three years.

Recently, a rare and devastating rainfall and subsequent flooding killed scores of Djiboutians and displaced hundreds out of their meager homes. The Legionnaires are repairing the homes and other damage done by the storm, side by side with Marines who are operating a reverse-osmosis water purification unit that converts non-potable water to potable at the rate of 600 gallons an hour. All of these Marine Corps assignments fall under the combined authority of Marine Forces Pacific/Marine Central Command of Lt. Gen. Chip Gregson and Brig. Gen. Jerry McAbee, based on Oahu. Between the United States Marines and the Legionnaires in Djibouti, they well live up to the Legion's version of Semper Fidelis: "Honneur et Fidelité."

P.T. Brent is a Hawaii businessman and a Marine infantry veteran who has been traveling with U.S. troops supporting Operation Enduring Freedom.

There is no other love
that can match the quintessential love
of one drunken Marine for another.

Marine General James Mattis

Chapter 15 is dedicated to Jim Sharp, the man who "patiently" taught
P.T. to swim the oceans of the world.

Keep setting records, Iron Man Kimo.

15

The Japanese Alamo, aka Alamo in the Pacific

Editor's note: originally published in the "Star-Bulletin" on Sunday, 9 May 2004

First, a personal reflection . . .

My mom and I had just exited the Strand Theater on Division Street (Polish Area) in Chicago one warm summer night. Mom, with quiet pride asked, "Did you know that Robert Brent, the man I am about to marry, was a Marine?"

I was 8 years old and the next day, I asked if he had been on Iwo Jima with John Wayne. The movie, "Sands of Iwo Jima," had left a lasting impression on then Patrick Monaghan. I walked home thinking what an incredible and brave man this future stepfather must be. Perhaps he was even cooler than the "Duke." I vowed to follow in his footsteps

after I outgrew my Buster Brown shoes.

Years later, while at Little Creek, Virginia, with the 2nd battalion, 24th Marines, I remember climbing down a cargo net, laden with military paraphernalia into a Higgins boat, which was smashing against the side of a Navy 558-foot LSD. The experience was intimidating; unlike "The Sands of Iwo Jima," there was no patriotic Marine's hymn being played in the background, like there had been for Sergeant John Stryker.[59] Military adventures in real life are far removed from the silver screen. During that time, I also was teaching Marine Corps history classes at the Reserve Center, and Iwo Jima was always a major study.

A few days ago, I stepped off a private charter at Iwo Jima. The rush of getting there (no easy mission) was over, and my energy had faded. Left were some inner feelings, almost impossible to describe. Never have two such extraordinary warrior groups fought so bitterly for such a small, bleak place. Their nobility and the sacrifices would rest heavily on any visitor's mind, perhaps a little more so, for a Marine type. These memories from third grade onward called and asked for this record.

The Japanese Alamo

Question: Where in the world is P.T.B.?

Answer: Lat/Long 24.3 North, 141.5 East, Elevation 528 feet

A miniscule island comprised of only seven and one half square

---

[59] In the film, "The Sands of Iwo Jima," John Wayne played Marine Sergeant John Stryker.

miles, Iwo Jima is smaller than Santa Monica, California. It is about twice the size of Honolulu Harbor and approximately two-thirds the size of Pearl Harbor. From the sky in a Marine Corsair, this sulfuric volcanic island is dramatically different from what was experienced by Marine infantry on these black coral beaches.

Iwo Jima[60] experienced another invasion this month. Marines based on Okinawa landed in full force on a training mission. Marines are long on training, but the battles they've won prove their methods effective. Green Beach, just below Mount Suribachi (556 tough feet), is far less lethal to Marines today than it was to their predecessor Leathernecks 59 years ago. Then, Iwo's black coral sand swallowed the men up to their knees, immobilizing them.

Fifty-nine years ago, Marine and Navy pilots called it "a charred pork chop." A task force of 495 ships assembled offshore, more than our current Navy now has in totality (about 300 ships), awaiting orders to "land the landing force." The 3rd, 4th and 5th Marine Divisions encountered horrific casualties when attacking this now legendary rock. The results were incomprehensible losses to both the Japanese and the Americans alike. Over 40,000 casualties were suffered by both sides, including the 28,000 killed in action. Eighty-two Medals of Honor[61] were awarded in WWII; twenty-seven of those were earned on Iwo Jima alone.

One MOH was awarded to PFC Jack Lucas, who conned Marine

---

[60] Japanese for Sulfur Island
[61] Medal of Honor abbreviation is MOH.

recruiters into an enlistment at the age of 14. PFC Lucas had been a stowaway on the troop transports and turned seventeen while on Iwo. This baby Marine fell upon two grenades and subsequently survived 27 surgeries. When asked why he took such a risk, Jack replied, "to save my buddies."

Joe Fachet is back on Iwo for the first time since he fought there. Joe, when he first arrived as a replacement Marine, asked a corporal why a man was out there amongst the Marine bodies with bullets flying all around him. The corporal replied, "He is Father Pat Lonergan, our chaplain, giving last rites to the men." With tears running down his cheeks, Joe Fachet says that until the day he dies, he believes he saw a halo of safety around Father Lonergan.

We join seven other Iwo Jima veterans who have returned. Ranging from 77 to 85, these aging Leathernecks are all here for a last visit. Their first and only time back since 1945, these men will, for a final moment, revisit this hallowed island, now a shrine to both sides.

These somber men speak softly and profoundly . . .

"Not a day in my life goes by I do not think of Iwo," says Joe Fachet.

"A rough place to be," says Jim Platt of Buffalo, New York.

When asked why he went, Marine Platt's answer is simple. "I'm a Marine; we go where we are sent and do what they tell us to do. We do not go home until the job gets done."

"It was kill or be killed. I feel at times, maybe, I never should have left here alive," is the sentiment of Charles Modrell of Kansas City.

"It made a better man out of me," states Al Abbatiello, who hails from the Bronx, NYC.

Long after the battle ended, the Japanese commander, General

Bill Leverence, age 85, and son Mike, age 55, from Chicago, show Bill's now famous Iwo flamethrower photograph. Bill, wounded on Iwo, finally returned for a last reflective moment.

Kuribayashi, received high accolades from Lt. General Smith of the Marine Forces. Smith lavished praise on this amazing Japanese military man. Smith stated that Kuribayashi fought better than the Germans or any foe we had ever fought in WWII. General Kuribayashi was educated in the USA. He was quoted as stating, "The United States is the last country in the world that Japan should ever fight."

Alamo in the Pacific

For the Japanese and their commanding general, this was their Alamo. Iwo Jima is just 660 miles from Tokyo. The mayor of Tokyo was also the mayor of this same prefecture with two critical airfields. The USA was attacking their homeland. Just like the Texans, General Todamuchi Kuribayashi had been ordered to hold off the invaders of his homeland as long as possible. Like the Alamo, he was tasked with fighting to the last man. This strategy would make the cost so dear to the Marines that his hope was that the United States might negotiate rather than invade Japan.

Like the Alamo, the Japanese Army fought until virtually every one of 22,000 troops had died, including 30 children—each was issued two grenades, one to attack Marines and the other for self destruction. There is a monument on Iwo for these young botany students who were stranded on this sulfuric island. The Marines, for the first time, had higher casualties than the enemy. Twenty-four thousand Marines were killed or wounded. To look at it another way, two out of every three Marines who landed on Iwo were killed or wounded. The transport ships, which were crowded upon arrival, departed Iwo Jima with ample room on board for all of the somber men returning home.

The general had spent a year building, arguably, the most impenetrable fortress of all time, comprised of a series of caves from 30 to 75 feet below the rock surface. Many days of naval fire and air bombing resulted in few casualties. Only seven out of 22,000 were killed in attacks prior to D-Day. The Japanese were not on top of the island. Indeed, they were "inside" it. Lighting systems, ventilation shafts, and 400 beds carved into the rock walls constituted their hospital. The tunnels all were interlaced so their murderous artillery and mortar fire would descend upon the Marines throughout these horrific battles. As one Marine said, "Not getting hit was like running through rain and trying to stay dry."

General Kuribayashi admonished his men to kill 10 Americans each before they died for the emperor. The Japanese were completely out of water and food the last 10 days. Their night attacks on Marines showed all Marine canteens missing.

On 8 January 1949, the last two Japanese soldiers came out of these sulfur caves and surrendered to the American forces. They had read in a discarded paper that Americans were celebrating Christmas in Tokyo.

These Japanese soldiers were brave men who died at their posts; they were hated then, respected now. Today, those caves still have many ghostly military accouterments, which like the bodies of the defenders, have been mummified by this sulfuric heat. In 1984, Colonel Ripley of the Marine historical division discovered the journal of Kuribayashi and his chief of staff's body, all perfectly preserved.

1/400 of a second . . .

Over half a century later, each year, Marines (and they still are Marines) return to this black sand island where they lost 6,821 of their fellow Marines. These few aging warriors come once a year. They slowly climb up Mount Suribachi, where on D-Day plus four, 23 February 1945, in 1/400 of a second, Joe Rosenthal captured the combat picture of all time. It won the Pulitzer Prize. Five Marines and a Navy corpsman from the 28th Marine Regiment raised an oversized U.S. flag on a 100-pound, rusted plumbing pole. The flag (8 x 4 foot, ship's port flag), from an Hawaiian Based LST 779, was recovered from a ship damaged in the 7 December bombing of Pearl Harbor. The camera shutter blinked spontaneously as a Marine said, "There she goes." Now, the world's largest bronze sculpture is located in the nation's capital. The Corps icon was established for all time. In a Navy dark room in Guam, a photo technician, the first to see this Pulitzer Prize picture, wrote on the envelope . . .

The Unblinking Eye

In the blood-red light, the photo technician rolled up his sleeves, a pack of Lucky Strikes stuck snugly in the sleeve of one arm, and dipped down to lift the paper from the developer bath. His breath caught in his throat as he lifted the dripping image of five Marines and one Navy corpsman hoisting a shrapnel-torn but still rippling flag of the United States on top of Mount Suribachi. Trembling, he clipped the photograph taken by Joe Rosenthal to the line with rivulets running off in quiet, steady drops. When the picture dried, it was gently placed inside a manila envelope. It was titled simply and without description: "Here's one for all time."

The resulting Iwo Jima war bond drive set a never broken record—over $220 million was raised.[62] The three-cent postage stamp broke a record— $20 million in sales. The record for this unique vertical green stamp is still unbroken today.[63]

Three of the six flag-raisers died before leaving the island. Of the 40 Marines on the Suribachi assault platoon, only four survived. Our way of life in America, like freedom, is not cheap. On Iwo, we experienced a carnal and gruesome standard rarely witnessed since Gettysburg. "An ominous reminder to those who would wage war with the United States," stated John Ripley, the head of the Marine Corps history and traditions division.

Sadly, 1,500 WWII veterans die daily in the United States. All of these Marines are a salute to every U.S. fighting man who was ever sent off to war since 1776. Hopefully, Americans will always prove worthy of their sacrifices.

---

[62] That would be billions by today's standards.
[63] A first class postage stamp costs 46 cents today—still a good deal.

After securing the island, the Marine burial detail placed this sign at the cemetery for their fallen comrades . . .

When you go home
Tell them for us and say
For your tomorrow
We gave our today

Americans will forever be indebted to these humble heroes of yesteryear: the Marines of Iwo Jima.

COURTESY B. LINDSEY

Veteran Bill Leverence, 85, shown above with a Marine escort, stormed the Japanese island carrying a flame-thrower and became part of the Iwo Jima lore when he was captured.

About Iwo Jima

U.S. leaders wanted a base 660 miles from Tokyo for bombing and for crippled planes to be rescued. It had hundreds of miles of tunnels and was defended as homeland by the Japanese.

Now back in Japanese custody, it is jointly used in perpetuity by the U.S. Marines and Japan for military exercises. It is maintained as a shrine by the Japanese for their war dead.

Visit www.PacificWarMemorial.org for information about the Iwo Jima memorial at Marine Base Hawaii.

We have done so much with so little,
for so long; we now feel we can do
everything with nothing.

Colonel John Richard Bates, USMC
Ref: USMC's Tight Budget

A salute to a Marine infantryman from Chicago (WGC) who captained American jumbo jets across the globe and flew fighter jets as a Leatherneck colonel—Keep your head down, Sam Badiner.

16
The Grey Ghost

Editor's note: This article was originally published in the "Star-Bulletin" on Sunday 24 September, 2004

While Corporate America is jetting from one mega-deal to the next board meeting, the U.S. Marines have adapted the corporate jet for the war on terrorism. Considerably a leaner and meaner model, the Marines have taken a tornado-damaged G4, and for a third of the cost of the new executive version, converted it into a working member of the Corps' air power. This G4, based in Hawaii, has none of the luxurious amenities of its counterparts. It flies loaded down with pallets of supplies and gear and comes equipped with communications systems for war fighting. No luxuries can be found aboard; the Marines who use this jet even bring their own personal water and chow. The pace on board is 24/7 and would wear out the toughest of Fortune 500 executives. They land in far-off climes and exit with

The Grey Ghost

helmets, flak jackets and weapons at the ready. All this capability is at a fraction of the cost of a Corporate G4 model. The Grey Ghost, as this G4 is known, bears little resemblance to the famous Civil War General John Mosley.

Dateline: 29 August 2004 at 1745 hours, U.S. Marine Central Command Headquarters, MacDill Air Force Base, Florida. The C-20G, aka Gulf G4, takes off for Djibouti, Africa, via Nova Scotia, Canada, and Naval Base Italy (fuel stops). Cruising at 41,000 feet

with an all-Marine flight crew of seven Leathernecks (three in training), this aircraft transports senior Marine leadership (executives with 9mm pistols strapped to their hips) to and from the global war on

U.S. Marine General Jerry McAbee and his staff on the Grey Ghost enroute to Iraq

terrorism. There are eight Marine officers aboard heading to coordinate Marine operations in Africa, Afghanistan and Iraq. All are on mission critical assignments.

This aircraft that can fly at almost 90 percent of the speed of sound is based at Marine Corps Air Facility, Kaneohe Bay, Hawaii.[64] To date, in support of OEF/OIF, Grey Ghost crews have flown 476 sorties,

---

[64] Marine Corps Air Facility abbreviation is MCAF.

Grey Ghost portside

U.S. Marine General Jerry McAbee and his staff work on strategic plans enroute to Iraq.

1449 flight hours, 2004 passengers and 159,000 pounds of cargo.

The Grey Ghost has flown missions into virtually every country in the Central Command Area of Responsibility. This is a remarkable aircraft and crew tailored for the Marines and their requirements in the pursuit of the global war on terrorism.

P. T. Brent is a Hawaii businessman and U.S. Marine infantry veteran. He has been embedded with the Marines in Iraq and other conflict areas for the past 60 days.

War is life multiplied by some number that no one has ever heard of.

Sebastian Junger

"War"

Chapter 17 is dedicated to England's gift to the colonies, Adena Goodart, whose edits helped make many a story readable. There will always be an England.

17
Feature:
Dispatches From Afghanistan

Editor's note: This article was written for UPI on 10 September 2004.

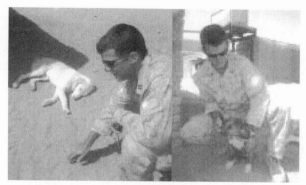

Fire Base Shkin, Afghanistan, Sept. 10 (UPI)—Meet the watchdogs of Fire Base Shkin: three liberated canines named Jarhead (the puppy), Sailor (white-sleepy one), and Chesty (not pictured). All three were adopted by the 14 Marines based at this outpost. Pictured with them is Capt. Jody Lynch.

Staff Sgt. Keith Gerena from Chicago loves these dogs but said he'd rather have a Home Run Inn Pizza from Chi-Town. Life, training, and patrols continue here, beneath these mountains, in a land where time and lifestyle are unchanged by the centuries. From the vantage point of the helicopter, all of the homes and buildings below look like beige sand castles.

Marine Capt. Jody Lynch meets our Black Hawk helicopter as we are dropped off in about 30 seconds at this remote firebase, only five kilometers from the Pakistani border. A short time on the deck will minimize the window of opportunity for anti-coalition militia to target the aircraft.

These Marine advisors are training the Afghan National Army, otherwise known as the ANA. Capt. Lynch says he would come back here in a New York minute, but his wife, Shelly, may want him home for a while first. Jody Lynch is an all-American guy from Mandeville, Louisiana. Jody once was recruited away by Ross Perot, but after two years, pulled every string possible to get his commission back, leaving the civilian world behind.

This captain and his commanding officer, Maj. Tom Clinton, believe the war in these mountains is being won. There are still a few Taliban around; last night's rocket attack proves it. The Marines responded with 105mm cannon, firing back 20 rounds within minutes. Capt. Lynch's patrol rushed up to the launch site, but the "bad guys" had used a timer to avoid the response and flown the coop.

Small units of al-Qaida fighters still fire rockets at the Afghan/coalition bases close to the Pakistan border when the mood hits them. The new Afghan National Army is holding the line though. Their men range from age 15 on up and are paid $5 to $7 a day. The morale of this new army is strong. They wear old U.S. Armed Forces uniforms and utilize captured Russian AK47 rifles.

The Marines like these fellows but do not trust local militia and laborers. Marines and ANA all live together in a three-mile circular compound. They eat Afghan food, which they prefer to American food. Rice, beans and mutton seem to be the mainstay. When Afghan soldiers eat MREs,[65] their mullah blesses the food after the ones containing pork are removed.

The Marines have learned to speak a little Dari—the Afghan dialect of Farsi, or Persian, and Pashto. The Afghan officers, led by Col. Ishaq, speak fair English, and classes are held nightly. When asked the whereabouts of Osama bin Laden, the ANA soldiers say they believe he is alive and in Pakistan.

However, they are in disagreement on whether the Pakistanis are harboring bin Laden. They know of the 9/11 tragedies and appear to have genuine anger. "These Afghans, for the first time, are seeing their own proud men in sharp uniforms—with the exception that this time, no one is robbing and abusing them," says Capt. Lynch.

To help establish cordial relations, the Marines have built schools and have dug wells, the two most-needed facilities. Lt. Col. Steve Morgan heads up a PRT,[66] tasked with bringing in these life-enhancing developments.

The schools we visited, one donated by a Japanese charity, had all the boys studying the three "R's." The primary challenge here is literacy. A day earlier, we attended a conference where Brig. Gen. Jerry McAbee carried a message to the provincial governor and the

---

[65] MREs = meals ready to eat
[66] PRT = provincial reconstruction team

local governor that his "big boss," Lt. Gen. Wallace C. Gregson, Commander of U.S. Marine Corps Forces in the Pacific, Pres. George Bush and the American people expected women to go to school and have their new rights respected. McAbee firmly reiterated his point. It turns out the general has three young granddaughters of his own.

Maj. Clinton finds that although the Afghanis may be 90 percent illiterate, they are innovative and clever in making this base work on an unbelievably minimal budget.

The national election on Oct. 9 will use pictures of the candidates, since most Afghans cannot read. This time the women will get to vote, and an astounding 41 percent are registered. In the Sharana Province, once the heart of Al-Qaida country, they are proud to announce that 48 percent of their women are registered.

"I hope the American people stay the course," says Capt. Lynch. "We are close, and patience should be the order of the day. Three thousand years of history will not be changed overnight."

I come in peace, I didn't bring artillery.
But I am pleading with you with
tears in my eyes:
If you fuck with me, I'll kill you all."

Marine General James Mattis (to Iraqi tribal leaders)

18

Interview With U.S. Marine General Jerry Mcabee

Editor's note: This story is from the author's "Combat Notebook: Dispatches from the War on Terrorism," 28 May 2004.

> *"For those who have fought for it, life has a special flavor the protected will never know."*

A few words written by an anonymous Marine, taken from a now famous combat ration box in Vietnam . . . and now echoed by the U.S. Marines in Afghanistan fighting a global war on terrorism. We are visiting the Marines arriving in AFG theater (Marine Expeditionary Unit) comprised of a fleet of Navy ships, aircraft and a battalion of over 1,000 U.S. Marines.

Tim Monaghan (pen name of Patrick Timothy Brent), left, traveling in Afghanistan, Qatar and Bahrain for an exclusive interview with Marine General Jerry McAbee, commanding general of Marine Base Hawaii in Kaneohe.

Quite a Proud Marine Family, the McAbees

Since 1936, a McAbee of Alabama has been serving America from within the U.S. Marine Corps. Brig. Gen. McAbee's father served in WWII and Korea, and his brother served in Vietnam. With retirement eminent, General McAbee simply states, "What better honor than to wear the uniform of the U.S. Marine for 35 years." The general served with Marine Commandant, General Norman Schwarzkopf during Desert Storm, and continues to serve in virtually every clime and place Marines might project their peace keeping force in readiness.

General Jerry McAbee is a southern gentleman who is the deputy component commander for U.S. Marine forces in the USCENTCOM theater. The general's duties take this Marine from his home at Kaneohe Marine Base in Hawaii to Afghanistan, Iraq and the network of countries which supply American resources to the war effort. We traveled with Brig. Gen. McAbee to Bahrain, Qatar and Afghanistan. He is well respected by his fellow Marines. He carries his own gear, lines up last for chow and is sure all Marines are taken care of prior to accepting something for himself. Clearly, this man still is a regular Marine. He shows a genuine empathy for these young Americans about to shove off for war. This is a hallmark and a quality found throughout the officers of our Marine Corps.

Interview

Hawaii Reporter: How are we training the Iraqis to fend for themselves?

The General: The new Iraq army is established, so is the Iraq Civil defense; and the Iraqi police were all carefully selected post-war. They appear to have taken the mission seriously, and many have died fighting these extremists.

Hawaii Reporter: What is your forecast for Iraq in the next five years?

The General: Iraq is a rich country, they have educated people and resources, i.e., the second largest supply of oil in the world, a fine infrastructure, good roads, ample lakes, rivers and water for agriculture—all representing a bright future. [Everything is] based on us keeping our resolve to provide security for this country which is so rich in history and culture. Two of the original wonders of the world are in Iraq.

Hawaii Reporter: Are the costs of lives and resources too costly?

The General: America's military has always fought outside America. They do this to defend our way of life. WWII was to prevent direct invasion. This global war is to keep our way of life for our grandchildren and future generations. What we do here will define life in America for the next 50 years. Our young Marines know this, and our Corps pledged to accomplish these goals.

We must stamp out poverty, ignorance and hatred. We need to help them have jobs, education and religious freedoms. Our Marines have sacrificed lives and limbs to make sure we stand now over here and not on our shores. It is a long investment. Americans well know that Freedom is *not* free.

Appeasing these people who attack our way of life is a poor investment. Churchill once said, "An appeaser is one who feeds the crocodile, hoping he will eat him last."

Hawaii Reporter: How are we doing in Iraq?

The General: The vast majority of Iraqi people just want the same thing we desire—jobs, religious freedom, to peacefully raise their families, and to be happy. A few people—foreign mercenaries, thugs, people who hate democracy, or in some cases, just hate westerners— hope to alter our resolve by terrorism. Most them are just self-seeking opportunists who wish for coalition forces to give up.

Hawaii Reporter: How is life today for Iraqis?

The General: All resources that serve the public are today superior to pre-war conditions—schools, hospitals, irrigation systems for agriculture, natural gas and oil at a record of 2.5 million barrels per day.

Hawaii Reporter: The ultimate outcome of this war?

The General: Our actions will define our American way of life for the next 50 years. We must stay the course.

P. T. Brent is a Hawaii businessman and former U.S. Marine infantry veteran. He has been embedded with the Marines in Iraq and other conflict areas for the past 60 days.

*From a Redleg (Artillery) to a pilot:
"Don't worry, we're using the
Big Sky/Little Bullet theory today."*

Salute to a Jarhead from Texas who thinks he is a Chinaman and has awesome ambitions.

19

Our Texas Air Force and a Few Hail Marys

Editor's note: from the author's "Combat Notebook: Dispatches from the War on Terrorism," 21 May 2004

Ground control to U.S. Air Force Hercules C-130

Sir: Condition Red . . . the field is under attack again.

Ground control: Advise taxi to bunker and evacuate the aircraft.

Captain: Request 14 right for take off.

Tower: Alfa, bravo, delta and fox trot sectors all under fire.

Co-pilot: Sir, tracer rounds at delta end of field.

Tower: Cannot comply sir unless you are declared take-off critical.

Captain: Runway 14 right now

From the Tech Sergeant in hold with 36 passengers:

Sir: rockets to rear of aircraft hitting.

Tower: Can you lift off before intersection delta?

Captain: Affirmative your last.

Tower: I am going to get a lot of s^#* over this . . .

Co-pilot: (starts reading a take-off check-list . . . rapidly.)

Captain: Keep moving Liz.

Pilot holding brakes then full power and a rapid accent to altitude.

Crew Chief: Sir: two rockets over our tail section . . . flares deploying.

Captain: Tower need to avoid the search chopper in area.

Tower: Chopper 17 stay under 200 feet.

Navigator: Have him at two o'clock.

Finally, a dramatic lift-off occurs under heavy fire at Balad Airfield Iraq, while this correspondent is riveted to the cockpit jump seat with his headset locked in to an intrepid and gripping real-life radio show. His helmet bag contains a notebook and penlight, and his hands are buried deep, noting the radio dialogue in a blacked-out cockpit.

A Hail Mary in 2.9 seconds

As one Marine put it . . . "I said many Hail Marys in 2.9 seconds . . ."

Departure was from Balad, the giant airfield that was once Saddam's pride, and is now called Anaconda by the U.S. Army, which operates an enormous supply and distribution operation from this besieged base for the Iraq theater of war. For better than two weeks, it has been targeted with live fire, most of which has been highly inaccurate. Its convoys are returning with KIAs and WIAs. The highways surrounding Anaconda belong to the Mahdi's private army. They control the highway using mortars, RPGs,[67] IEDs and SAF.[68]

The darkened C-130 climbs to 29,000 feet with only covert upper

---

[67] RPGs = rocket propelled grenades
[68] SAF = small arms fire

lights showing. The Hercules banks over the Tigris and Euphrates rivers on the edge of Baghdad and heads south safely with Marines, soldiers and national guardsmen heading home after a year in Iraq via the Kuwait relocation base.

Captain Ed Schindler, on furlough from American Airlines in Dallas, and his Texas National Guard crew have been in theater for 13 months now, flying Marines and supplies in and out of Iraq and Afghanistan. And what a crew it is! Tom Clancy could not have created a more competent and take-charge group of aviators. Lockheed-Martin builds these Hercules C-130s to perform combat take-offs under adverse conditions and execute critical landing in zones under fire.

They med-evac'ed some wounded Marines on their last mission. The navigator, Captain Gary Kerr, spotted the chopper and kept them out of zones under fire, in unison with Tech Sergeant Anne Witcher, a commercial pilot back in the USA. The cargo crew, Tech Sergeants Blyane Leach and Ken Shartzer, kept the passengers advised and spotted the incoming rockets.

President George W. Bush, another Texas National Guard aviator, would have been proud of this crew from Crome 22 Texas. (Perhaps they have more time in service than their commander-in-chief.)

The C-130 banked in a moonlit night sky filled with Arabian stars, picked up a heading of 129 magnetic, flew over a string of wells brilliantly illuminated in oil-rich southern Iraq, and followed a bright

Kuwait highway to a safe haven.

The joint team of USAF, Marines and other armed services branches are all comprised from one common denominator. They are all American patriots who want to bring a better life to some people in a far-away land.

P.T. Brent is a Hawaii businessman and U.S. Marine infantry veteran. He has been embedded with the Marines in Iraq and other conflict areas for the past 60 days.

Of all the many titles, monikers and positions I've held in my most fortunate life, the appellation "Marine" has always meant the most.
It should be easy to understand.
Why? Jobs and sports are fine, but the United States Marine Corps stands for something: honor, courage and commitment—and they mean it.
Ask Colonel Walt Ford or any Leatherneck. They know.

P.T. Brent, 10 November 2011

MSG Peking Ball

20

Interview With Maui Marine Ernest Hoopii

Editor's note: from the author's "Combat Notebook: Dispatches from the War on Terrorism," 3 June 2004

fghanistan: Meet First Sergeant Ernest Hoopii, United States Marine Corps. Hoopii is a career Marine from Maui. Back during high school years on Oahu, his pals at Mid-Pacific used to call him "Hoop" as he demonstrated his athletic prowess at volleyball, track, and of course, hoops.

Only a few Marines now know him as "Hoop." The young Marines at Charlie Company reverently call him First Sergeant. He is older and perhaps wiser than any man in the unit. Hoop holds a position of considerable esteem within the Corps. He is the highest-ranking enlisted man in this infantry company of over 200 men. The younger company commander,

Ernest Hoopii (left), a Marine from Maui, with Tim Monaghan in Afghanistan.

a Captain Paul Merida from Oakland, relies on Hoop's leadership, maturity, and respect with the young Marines. Most are going into harm's way for the first time, a memory and experience these Leathernecks will keep for a lifetime, but an experience their protected loved ones will never have to know. The United States has always chosen to fight our enemies overseas before they reach our shores.

This hapa haole boy (Hawaiian and Portuguese), now a veteran Marine from Maui, is wise beyond his years. After working in security at the Hyatt Regency, Hoop joined the Marines. Why? When asked, Hoop responds that the Beirut bombing really upset[69] him. His dad had been a Marine in Korea. After Beirut, Hoop immediately called a Marine recruiter in Oahu and went off to boot camp at the San Diego recruit depot.

Hoop's priorities are to accomplish the mission assigned while taking care of his fellow Marines, win the hearts of the Afghans, and seek out/neutralize the people who wish to kill Americans as well as Afghans desiring freedom. This is not without sacrifice. Hoop's wife, Jeane Maria, is back at Lejeune (Luh jern) with Sean and Justin, awaiting their dad's safe return. Hoop misses them. He also misses his new Harley purchased while at sea, and fishing and eating poi with pals in Maui. However, Hoop says, "Once we are done in Afghanistan, we can roll right down to Iraq on our way home and

---

[69] Hoop actually did not say upset; the author substituted upset for another word.

clean it up too."

These young men may shove off for the usual patriotism, adventure, duty and honor. However, when rounds are fired in anger, Marines fight for each other. They endure, not for lofty principles, but because they truly are their brother's keeper. Simply stated . . . they fight for their fellow Marines. Hoop's leadership will be a critical lifesaver when his company is under fire.

Since the 1900s, skeptical people have said, "Tell it to the Marines," meaning that they believe Marines are an omniscient outfit that will separate reality from the foolish stories (sea stories). The rumors (scuttlebutt) say Americans are targets in Afghanistan and that winning the hearts and minds of the local populace is impossible. Well, don't "tell it to the Marines" of Charlie Company. These warriors are the best the United States has. Under the leadership of Maui's First Sergeant "Hoop," they have been commissioned with winning the hearts and minds of the Afghan people, while vigorously pursuing any enemy types who wish to alter and embarrass the peace mission.

These young Marines know that Afghanistan is better off than it was two years ago when another group of Leathernecks secured the dirt airstrip at "RHINO." They immediately covered about 40 miles to pay a call on the Taliban at their capital at Kandahar. A bitter battle ensued, but the base is now in coalition forces' custody.

Afghan schools, hospitals, utilities and resources are better than they have ever been in the history of the country. A new highway that will loop the country together is currently under construction.

Americans, indeed, are fortunate to have First Sergeant Hoopii and his Marines fighting for democracy. This would be a most auspicious moment to take pride in the United States and our forces overseas. Do you remember pride in our country? We used to have it by the carload. Forget whether or not you agree with taking on Osama bin Laden. Just get yourself a flag and wave it proudly. Let's pray for our distant warriors, and let's bring our young Americans home safely.

The faces of these young warriors may appear to be younger. Faces like those of Paul Merida and Joe Silvio. Yes, the faces may appear younger. But beneath those faces runs the same blood that stained and won battlefields from Tripoli to Iwo Jima, and from Guadalcanal to Iraq. Their packs, their rifles . . . they weigh as much. The heat, dust, cold, and long night marches are all still there. They are the same outfit. The United States Marine Corps.

P. T. Brent is a Hawaii businessman and U.S. Marine infantry veteran. He has been embedded with the Marines in Iraq and other conflict areas for the past 60 days.

Boys, the honeymoon's over.
From now on, you're Marines.

Major Geoffrey Caton
from the movie "Wake Island" (1942)

Chapter 21 is dedicated to Frances Gates: words fail to do justice to this extraordinary woman. Her gifted staffing of countless Irish, polo and gyrene projects made life a little better for all who were fortunate to know this kind and charming lady.

21
Wake Island

Imagine, a time machine transporting you back into 1941!

First stop—Wake Island, 19° 182 03 N, 166° 382 03 E—a tiny coral atoll 2,300 miles west of Hawaii, named after Captain William Wake of the British Empire. You are aboard a Pan Am Clipper ship[70] with the call sign "China Clipper," and the sun is shining on its 130-foot wingspan.

PLOOOOSH! Your plane's pontoons gently set down in a crystal clear, tropical lagoon protected by coral reefs. You flashed over the international dateline after departing Midway Island eight hours earlier. Your clipper ship taxis to Wake Island to refuel, where you disembark on a dock in front of the Pan Am Hotel for a rest, before continuing on to Manila, or another tropical destination for a vacation filled with diving, fishing and golf. Aboard your aircraft are 14 passengers; among them are an Army Air Corps colonel assigned to General MacArthur's staff in the Philippines, businessmen, and affluent people on holiday. All of them, indeed, are stopping at a small

---

[70] A Martin Aircraft M-130

slice of tropical paradise made priceless by three factors: location, location, location.

Pacific transitioning by air or water, refueling, and rest would all have been improbable without this tiny atoll wisely claimed by the United States in 1899.

This is precisely why the Empire of Japan made it their second surprise strike at the same time they struck Pearl Harbor on 7 December 1941. The Japanese Navy assigned this mid-Pacific atoll high priority. They believed they could seize it in a day or two. The Japanese planners overlooked one compelling factor. The First Marine Defense Battalion defended this critical post in the mid-Pacific. The Marine Corps charged the enemy a heavy price for this miscalculation during the next 15 days. Two dozen Japanese airplanes were shot down; two destroyers and one submarine were sunk, and nearly 1,000 invading soldiers were killed in action.[71]

On 23 December 1941, Marines had just killed over 50 invading Japanese troops and had two prisoners tied to a tree when they saw a Japanese Navy officer along with Commander Winfield Cunningham marching up with a white flag of surrender. They mistakenly believed the Japanese had surrendered. These Leathernecks had crushed every landing attempted by the Japanese at various beaches on the atoll. Sadly, faced with no reinforcements and supplies, the Navy commanding officer had decided to surrender

---

[71] Only 52 United States Marine Corps casualties in the first 15 days of battle.

the island. The Marines were stripped naked; their hands were tied with wire behind their backs, and they marched to a spot of execution. A Japanese officer halted the execution and sent them and most of the civilian workers to slave labor camps in China and Japan. Later in 1943, Admiral Sakaibara ordered 98 remaining civilian workers executed. After the Marine Corps returned to Wake Island, Admiral Sakaibara was tried and hung as a war criminal.

Mr. Leslie Demarest Enderton, Executive Director, Oahu Visitors and father of an infantry Marine/scout sniper, captured this outstanding shot of the USMC memorial at Wake Island.

The first Marine Medal of Honor of WWII was awarded posthumously to Captain Hank Elrod, VMF-211, for having shot down two Japanese Zero fighters, sinking a Japanese Destroyer, landing his crippled F4 Wildcat fighter back at Wake, and dying while fighting the invasion as an infantry Marine.

Now take the Time Machine forward to today—2010:

This past week, our Air Force's Pacific Command General Gary North, a gentleman from Virginia, invited this writer and a three other community leaders to join him on an Air Force C-17 transport supply plane to Wake Island, where Air Force commander, Major Aaron Wilt hosted a jam-packed inspection of the facilities, including a visit to the historical spots on the island. The civilian/contract side of the island is under the direction of a United States Marine Corps veteran Wayne White. This Wake Island project manager respects the awesome history of Wake Island Leathernecks and manages to keep all facilities in fine shape for the U.S. Air Force's critical missions at Wake, which range from refueling to missile and radar defense of the Pacific Command. This 2.9 square mile rock in the middle of the world's largest ocean is an outstanding representation of our Air Force's commitment and of the dedicated project personnel who sacrifice much to serve America's interest in the Pacific.

Bravo Zulu Wake Island!

General Gary North (four stars), CG of USAF Pacific Command,
and P.T.B.

Being ready is not what matters.
What matters is
winning after you get there.

Lt. General Victor H. Krulak, USMC
April 1965

22

Triple Zero One
A day in the life of a combat Marine

Editor's note: This story was originally published in the "Honolulu Star-Bulletin" and was later printed in the Pentagon's "Early Bird" publication.

Zero zero zero one . . . It is one minute after midnight Saturday on a wind-swept rooftop overlooking Husaybah, Iraq. Staff Sergeant Adam Walker looks out, during a quiet moment, at the scene where his platoon lost some good men yesterday. Tired, but unable to sleep, he remembers he has not eaten in nearly a day. Adam writes back home, "The intensity here is contagious. We have been bloodied and the anger is big time. Losing is not in the vocabulary of these Marines. There is a warrior spirit here, which is hard to explain to many of you folks back home."

0100 Dogs are barking constantly . . . the damn local dogs are unnerving. When on patrol, the stealth vision lenses are compromised by the dogs' relentless barking. There are always anywhere from three to 10 dogs barking. They give away your position . . . you often know where another Marine patrol is by the sound of the dogs. They do not bark at locals . . . their smell is different.

0130 Adam removes his K-bar knife from its sheath, located on the front of his new flak jacket. The new SAPI[72] plates now stop 7.62 rounds, the bullets of the AK 47, the preferred weapon of his enemies. They are heavier, but their stopping power saves lives. The percentage of WIA versus KIA[73] is six to one. The military aide stations and hospitals have worked around the clock lately. His K-bar slices the length of an MRE[74] pouch—spaghetti and meatballs served cold. The packet includes a heat thermal pouch, which, with an inch of water, heats the food fairly well. For Marines in a tactical position, there is little time or interest in heat. Adam takes a plastic spoon and scoops out a few bites of chow, remembering the sign at the base mess hall—"Great place to dine . . . ten thousand flies cannot be wrong"—just as his platoon commander, 2nd Lt. Tom Prentice, arrives to pass on the latest "gouge."[75]

Last night at the mess hall in Iraq, the TV was tuned to CNN, and journalists were once again talking about the abuse of prisoners in Iraq. Sergeant Jerry Butzen yelled, "Turn that F$%!ing thing off!". Marines believe these were dangerous men they sent to prison. They do not deserve to be back on the streets, where they will be planting more explosives to kill Americans.

---

[72] SAPI = self armor protection inserts
[73] wounded-in-action = WIA; killed-in-action = KIA
[74] MRE = meal ready to eat
[75] Gouge is Marine-speak for data-scoop, etc.

0200   With his M16 tucked into his poncho liner bag only halfway in order to keep it M16 at the ready, Adam slowly wakes to thoughts of home. He was dreaming of a pretty girl name Kathy. As reality sets in, Adam thinks about the recruiter he met in high school. Where is he now? The grizzled Marine gunnery sergeant asked him if he thought he had the stuff to become a Marine. Well, if the old Gunny could be here now, Adam believes he might pass muster.

Marines near Fallujah, Iraq, remain watchful after fending off an attack by insurgents, while children nearby seem unperturbed.

0500   Corpsman Steve Colon, a Navy guy, affectionately called "Doc," drops in to report that all supplies have arrived. The U.S. Navy provides all medical personnel for Marines.[76] Every Marine is a basic rifleman; even the aviators, cooks, and truckers are riflemen. Even the JAG lawyer, Major Laura Monaghan, is trained in infantry. No one is a noncombatant. This is the way it has always been with the Marines.

0530   Adam pulls out his combat notebook. Plans are for a patrol later in the day into Fallujah. Now is the time for a few moments for personal hygiene. Marines shave each and every day. An unshaven Marine hopefully has just returned from patrol. It is a discipline—one of the many by which Leathernecks live.

Empty cartons from the MREs are often used as crude portable toilets. Baby wipes and a personal supply of toilet paper from back

---

[76] The Marine Corps is a Department of the Navy.

home are prized. Mail call (about twice a week) is one of the few work details that always has many volunteers. There are some porta-johns—always with a line; there are lines for chow, lines for mail, and lines for new gear.

0600   After a few more hours of shut-eye, slumber is interrupted by the constant slamming of the door of their hardback tent. BAM! BAM! After all, it is only a plywood door with a bungee cord. BAM! BAM! Adam gets the platoon up for chow and for weapons cleaning. M16s, rocket launchers, SAWs,[77] and AT4s[78] all have to be 100 percent clean. The Marines work in small fire team units of four and are inspected several times by senior NCOs.[79] Lance Corporal Rich Lindsay is worried about his ACOG new sniper scope; training is scheduled. Marines are long on training, training, and re-training.

1100   The radio echoes a message now seared to his memory forever. Marines are receiving SAF[80] and mortars from the town; five Marines are dead and nine are wounded. The enemy has new ideas like frozen mortars. Mortar rounds are placed with water in PVC pipes until frozen, then positioned at angles to hit Marines later, as the sun beats down and releases the round in the tube.

Fear hits! An RPG[81] flies within inches of his head; shrapnel from it cuts his cheek. Adam tucks his head down and wishes he could

---

[77] SAWS = squad automatic weapons
[78] AT4s = anti-tank weapons
[79] NCOs = non-commissioned officers
[80] SAF = small arms fire
[81] RPG = rocket-propelled grenade

pull his helmet down to his toes as rounds hit. The brawl has started again. Adam hears PFC Dick Moore yell, "The f#$&%*g Hagiis are on the roof. We need some grenades on there f#$%&*g fast!" The air is thick with the smell of cordite.[82]

1300 The Skipper (company commander) Captain Chris Bronzi brings a platoon up to flank the insurgents and radios in for a Cobra to fire on the roof. Suddenly, all is quiet; and we create a casualty collection point and call in med-evac. Everyone is counted, security checked, and new zones of fire are soon established.

1500 Mail arrives, as some Marines return from the Internet bunker, where they wait about an hour to secure 30 minutes on a computer for e-mail from home. The news is filled with the prison photos and ill treatment of Iraqi prisoners. Some of these prisoners were captured by Adam's unit while setting up IEDs to kill Americans. The sergeant major says, "One 'oh shit' like this takes away from the 100 good things Marines do in the field every day." Adam thinks that now many will believe this handful of prison guards represents all Americans. "Damn!" Corporal John Redmond jokes, "We can get even with these Hagiis by sending all of their women to college. Then they will get the same treatment American men get."

Last week Marines rebuilt a medical clinic and a local school. Jobs have been created for hundreds of locals in their AOR. Locals are turning in these insurgents by the dozen, as they, too, are tired of the

---

[82] Cordite is gunpowder.

conflict. The press often fails to note the good that has been accomplished. Iraq is setting records for hospitals, schools and an improved standard of life. As for the locals, three-quarters of them seem to welcome the Marines; the problem is knowing which ones to trust. Most Iraqis are happy Saddam is gone, but they have been raised to dislike westerners as well as people of different faiths.

When Marines are on patrol, kids come out and wave; men just stand around drinking chai and staring. You wave and sometimes you get a smile and a "Haloe Mister." You rarely see women; if you do, they are covered except for their dark eyes (often beautiful ones) staring at you. We never wave to the women. So much for the land of flying carpets, harems, slave dens, Ali Baba and Sinbad the sailor. All are now bygone fantasies.

1600   The squad links up with Lieutenant Rustin Bates's CAAT[83]; several armored vehicles are firing at the squad. Lt. Bates has the Marines fire AT4s and Tows at the enemy, under cover of his men's rifles. He rushes the vehicles and drops a fragmentation grenade into three vehicles, making a combat roll after each grenade drop to avoid getting hit.

1630   Back at a vehicle checkpoint, a white Mercedes Benz is seen approaching at high speed. Without hesitation, Lt. Bates draws his 9mm pistol and fires two rounds into the high-speed car. The vehicle pulls over, and the three occupants are detained.

---

[83] CAAT = combined arms anti-tank platoon

1700   The Marines have some hot chow brought up in VAC cans[84] from the mess; some watch movies on personal DVD players. The unit was back at its home base in the USA only four months after the initial war last year. This time, considerably smarter and saltier, most of them brought over a few creature comforts.

1800   Late afternoon is spent preparing for another patrol. Maps, "comm." and assignments are covered and reviewed in painstaking detail. One fire team is doing laundry by hand shaking it in old ammo cans with some soap and rocks. They squeeze in personal hygiene as time permits.

The weather is picking up. This part of Iraq is like the high desert of Afghanistan where Adam served two years ago. It's just like 29 Palms California; the winds are ferocious and fine sand permeates everything. Wars have a tendency to locate in inhospitable places.

1900   Early evening. After a partial MRE, Adam tries to get some sleep, but thoughts of the upcoming patrol and the smells of Iraq keep him awake. Smells of rotting trash, stagnant water, human waste, oil soaked soil, body odors and cheap cigarettes give Iraq a unique stench of its own. Iraqis burn all of their trash openly— plastics, foods, everything. It all offers a distinct odor; in time, you get inured to it. Gunny Vogt said that Iraq is like the world's largest ashtray turned upside down.

2200   And the patrol assembles. Adam believes this war will

---

[84] VAC cans = vacuum cans

reaffirm his Corps' reputation for fighting success, or his Marines will die trying. He knows that whenever he has been nervous about young Marines, they have always far surpassed his expectations. Adam has one of his squads gather around him as he kneels and prays

. . .

2300 "Lord, we pray you will grant us success. We are Marines; bring us all back safely. The Lord's work will be done this day. Amen."

Most Marines believe their appointed time to leave this world is set and there is little they can do to change it.

2329 Iraq has the same rain, dust, fear and death that make all wars costly wastes and experiences best not shared or wished upon any man. All military men have experienced it, ever since Alexander the Great.

2359 One minute until midnight. Another day has passed for these Marines from 3rd Battalion, Seventh Marines Regiment.

Proud footnote: Lt. Bates has been awarded the Bronze Star with Combat V for valor.

P.T. Brent is a Hawaii businessman and a Marine veteran who traveled with U.S. troops supporting Operation Enduring Freedom. This article is the author's salute to Eddie Sherman, Hawaii journalist and World War II Pearl Harbor veteran.

Volume V

LEATHERNECK

Many thanks to everyone at "Leatherneck" magazine
for allowing me to reprint the following stories, for their
cooperation and support, and for the fine job that they do
on a daily basis.

P.T.B.

Self-respect leads to self-discipline. When you have both firmly under your belt, that's real power.

Clint Eastwood

A salute to Colonel Walt Ford editor/publisher of MCA's "Leatherneck" magazine and an exceptional gentleman who motivates and inspires all who work with him.

Diplomats in Blue
Hong Kong's "China Marines"

By P.T. Brent

One of the more exotic postings for Marine security guards (MSGs) must be the United States Consulate General, Hong Kong and Macau. Jockeying to grab the opportunity to protect United States interests and the consulate staff in this former British colony are a few of America's finest young men and women serving in today's United States Marine Corps.

Under duress, the Chinese Emperor ceded these lands to the British "Foreign Devils" in 1842. The 29-square-mile island, 1,000 yards from mainland China, became a jewel in Queen Victoria's crown and dazzled the world for 150 years.

Hong Kong, also known as the "fragrant harbor," is a unique post of the Corps. Life on and near the South China Sea remains an adventure. In that cornucopia of life, East meets West.

To understand more of the area requires a return to an era when the fabled Gurkha Brigade trained, while the Brits and their "Yank" pals played polo in the New Territories. James Clavell's best-selling novels "Tai-Pan" and "Noble House" (based on the Jardene Matheson Corporation, once the most powerful trading company in

Marine security guards enjoy frequent opportunities to meet and host visiting American and foreign dignitaries. Here, then-Deputy Secretary of State John Negroponte (third from right) meets with Marines in Hong Kong. (Note: Department of State Diplomatic Security guidance precludes naming the Marines in the photo due to operational security concerns.)

the Far East) are fascinating, dramatic and realistic tales about Hong Kong and surrounding areas. Marine security guards are exposed routinely to the history of those times and places.

A historical anomaly, Hong Kong has defied all odds and triumphs to this day. A compact island community, Hong Kong has 6.9 million people living in an area the size of Phoenix. It is clearly the most compact commercial and entrepreneurial location in the world. Its mysterious Chinese culture, forever married to British colonial history, has matured Hong Kong into a flourishing international trade center.

The rock island and its "Happy Valley" have become the world's most dramatic shopping center, a cement jungle where skyscrapers soar, filling every cubic inch of space with people and business. Not easily described, Hong Kong is a distillation of trade, energy and unbridled power.

On July 1, 1997, the British colonialists lowered the "Union Jack" for the last time and the United Kingdom relinquished the island colony to the People's Republic of China. It is now a special administrative region under the "one country,

Keeping fit is what Marines do, and the Hong Kong Marines take advantage of the demanding terrain to challenge themselves.The author, P.T. Brent (far left), joins detachment leathernecks for a good run.

two systems" principle, a brilliant British diplomatic achievement that seems to be working. The leathernecks assigned to the post recognize the history of the area and make every effort to learn even more about the rich history of the region. While travel is encouraged, a low profile is the order of the day at this post and others outside of the United States.

Among the Marines in the Marine Security Guard Detachment is Sergeant Bernard Epps. From Philadelphia, "Bernie," like most

Marines, has been to Iraq, gaining combat experience with a Marine expeditionary unit. Epps is in charge of the mess at the Marine House. Much like in shipboard officers' dining facilities, MSG Marines must organize, inventory and control the funds necessary to operate their household, and Sgt Epps does that very well.

Sgt Joe Nunley, a watchstander from Oceanside, Calif., knows Marine history cold. A solid Marine, prior to MSG duty, he earned the Sentry of the Year Award at Marine Corps Base Camp Pendleton, Calif. Also at Pendleton, Nunley took on special details, including participation in President Ronald Reagan's burial ceremony.

Nunley is the detachment's morale, welfare and recreation non-commissioned officer. He is, therefore, in charge of social events, such as the gatherings at the Marine House. The gatherings provide proceeds to help finance the detachment cultural and historical-awareness outings and the annual Birthday Ball. The Marine Birthday Ball is the major event scheduled for any embassy or consulate, including Hong Kong.

Sgt Cavel Wallen, from the Bronx, is assistant detachment commander. She also is a gourmet cook and frequently prepares her native Jamaican specialty, oxtail stew, for the detachment. Wallen stays in shape and looks like a blur when running up the steep, 1,800-foot Victoria Peak. After completing MSG School, she served at two other MSG posts prior to Hong Kong.

Sgt Sergio Gonzalez from Downey, Calif., deployed to Iraq prior to MSG training. He, too, is on his third posting. "I want to get back to the Fleet Marine Force," said this Marine who routinely scores 300, the maximum

COURTESY OF GYSGT DAT NGUYEN

Detachment members, along with Consulate employees and staff, conduct an expansive and productive Toys for Tots program in Hong Kong as demonstrated during this 2008 toy-wrapping evening.

score, on his physical fitness test.

Originating from Buffalo, N.Y.'s chilly climes, Sgt Ian Minard is the training NCO for the detachment. Minard deployed during Operation Iraqi Freedom in 2004 prior to being accepted to MSG School. He is another member of the detachment who is on his final MSG posting prior to returning to his regular duties.

Providing senior leadership to this MSG detachment is the detachment commander, Gunnery Sergeant Dat Nguyen, who, like most senior Marine NCOs, is meticulous in his professional demands, but also always takes care of his Marines.

Originally from Vietnam, GySgt Nguyen is assisted by his wife with his more informal duties. Only detachment commanders may be married while on MSG duty. The detachment commander's wife assists in a wide range of activities, often acting as the detachment's social and protocol adviser, uniform inspector and counselor/mentor for the younger watchstanders.

Colonel Jim Holman, USMC (Ret.), now a Hong Kong business executive, said, "Being a detachment commander is one of the most difficult Corps assignments. It is the only chance a staff noncommissioned officer has of being commanding officer of Marines without his boss getting shot."

GySgt Nguyen enjoys the leadership challenges and taking advantage of every opportunity to support the U.S. mission in one of the truly exotic postings for a Marine.

Editor's note: If you are an active-duty Marine and think you may want to try your hand at this independent duty, see your career-retention specialist.

P.T. Brent, a former infantryman and frequent contributor to "Leatherneck," visited the detachment and prepared this story several months ago. It is good finally to acknowledge what our Marines are doing in Hong Kong.

Marine security guards are frequently transferred in and out, and the latest roster of MSG Marines in Hong Kong, as this issue went to the printer, included: GySgt Dat Nguyen, Det Cmdr; Sgt Andrew Adkins; Sgt Andrew Honeycutt; Sgt Chadwick Desseyn; and Sgt Nicholas Frenzer.

To serve is beautiful,
but only if it is done with a whole heart
and a free mind.

Pearl S. Buck

"The Dublin"
Embassy Marines in Ireland

By P.T. Brent • Photos by Hisako Orchid

The Marine Security Guard Detachment commander, SSgt Christopher Piazza, routinely coordinates with all the staff at the American Embassy in Dublin, including the ambassador. Ambassador Thomas Foley (seated) completed his service as United States Ambassador to Ireland on Jan. 22 of this year.

The French call it *je ne sais quoi:* an alluring and mysterious quality, one which lacks clear definition. Our Marines in Ireland understand it because they possess it. The Irish, of course, also have it; and, if you don't feel or "get it," you may never.

Think about it. Ireland's No. 1 export has been its gifted people. Throughout the world each and every year on March 17, everyone wishes he were Irish. A case in point: 21 U.S.

Presidents claim Irish heritage. Among those, Theodore "Teddy" Roosevelt claimed County Donegal, and Ronald Reagan claimed County Tipperary.

If this past November's 233rd Birthday Ball was any indicator, Marine security guard detachments are welcomed warmly in the magical land of leprechauns, shamrocks and Guinness. In a special moment that enhanced a memorable evening, Sergeant Cameron Baxter read the celebrated Birthday message by the 13th Commandant, General John Archer Lejeune (Luh jern), whose mother claimed Irish ancestry.

One reason this Ball was so flawless was the many hours of rehearsal on a cold and rainy tennis court, resulting in a perfect color guard the night of the Ball. Asked how long the color guard would be drilling in preparation, the detachment commander issued a typical Marine response: "Until they get it perfect."

American embassies and consulates worldwide proudly make November 10 a time to share the tradition of the U.S. Marine Birthday. The guest of honor at the Dublin Ball was Ambassador Thomas Foley. Other foreign embassies were in attendance, as well as an ebullient "expat" Marine contingent, including Father James Crofton, a graduate of Marine Corps Recruit Depot Parris Island, S.C., and now a parish priest in Dublin. Everyone came to honor America and the leatherneck tradition. Ambassador Foley said, "It is unbelievable. The long hours, the dedication and the good spirit we enjoy from our Marines here in Ireland."

Why is it such a distinctive event? One reason: It is Ireland, and, like all Marines, these embassy Marines make the Corps' Birthday a distinguished event. The Marines, with no financial support, commit their time to host one of the most tasteful Balls ever attended.

"The Dublin" aka "The Dub"

Embassy Marines in Ireland were awarded the title "The Dublin" in a spirit filled with good humor. They recently bested "The Hague," embassy Marines based in the Netherlands. "The Dublin" Marines publicly petitioned their commanding officer for the honor during a formal military dinner, held in Limerick, with the late Colonel John Ripley in attendance.

Hailing from Missouri City, Texas, Sgt Joel Powell, an aviation ordnance technician with the military occupational specialty (MOS) 6531, is a watchstander in Ireland. He joined the Corps in Houston after Sept. 11, 2001, because he "wanted to be with the best of the best. In two and one-half years I have been to 24 countries, and I get to live in a beautiful old mansion in Ireland."

At embassies around the world, the quarters that house detachment Marines are referred to as "Marine House" and are usually superb accommodations. Powell's first embassy was Vienna, Austria, then East Africa's Bujumbura, Burundi, with his last mission in Ireland. He is the supply noncommissioned officer for the detachment and proud to be part of The Dublin.

A Virginian, Sgt Andrew Kim (traffic management specialist, MOS 3112), stands Post One on his second MSG assignment. His first was Nicosia, Cyprus. Sgt Kim is in charge of the Marine House mess. He joined the Corps because he knew "Marines were the first into Iraq and Afghanistan and because President Reagan said: 'Marines make a difference.' "

"Marine House" Dublin provides facilities for exercising, including a swimming pool and weight room for the detachment, plus a setting for the occasional embassy staff social gathering.

Inset: The embassy's RSO, Michael Rohlfs (right), works closely with SSgt Piazza to coordinate internal and external security. Looking on is Janet Meyer, a former Marine captain, who also works at the embassy.

Prior to Marine Security Guard School, Sgt Baxter (helicopter crew chief, MOS 6174) was awarded two air medals in Afghanistan and authorized to wear the combat "V." The sergeant also worked recovery operations during hurricanes Katrina and Rita.

Why did Sgt Baxter join the Marine Corps? "I wanted to be with the best outfit." He told his friends back in Los Angeles: "Where else can I live in a $50 million mansion [Marine House, Dublin], interact with locals and learn a great deal on many subjects and get paid for it?" His first MSG post was Bamako, Mali, in West Africa. He is the assistant detachment commander for the Dublin Det.

Corporal Noel Bertrand is from Portland, Ore., with an administrative clerk occupational specialty, MOS 0121. After successfully completing the tough curriculum at MSG School, he headed to Doha, Qatar. During his second year, he was based at the embassy in Caracas, Venezuela, and now is serving on his final embassy assignment as the Dublin detachment's morale, welfare and recreation NCO and Birthday Ball NCO. Bertrand reflected: " 'The Dub' was a godsend. The detachment commander is outstanding, and the other Marines are awesome."

The newest arrival at Marine House, Ireland is Cpl Robert Spahn from Tampa, Fla., also an admin clerk. "When I enlisted, I did not want to mess around. The Marine recruiters told it square. MSG duty is a great step forward; we get a security clearance, Marine security guard duty offers good contacts, and the brotherhood at MSG is strong." This young corporal's first posting was Kuwait, and he is the training NCO in Dublin.

Staff Sergeant Christopher Piazza, an infantry (0369) Marine, has one of the best jobs in the Corps. He enlisted right after high school. Piazza has

SSgt Piazza and the Marines of the detachment are ably supported by Piazza's Marine veteran wife, Starr.

received two meritorious promotions and is a qualified Marine Corps martial arts instructor trainer.

Deployed to Nasiriyah, Iraq, and later assigned to the antiterrorism battalion at Camp Lejeune (Luh jern), N.C., he then deployed to the U.S. Embassy/Green Zone in Baghdad. Accompanied by his family, he is on the first of two tours as an MSG detachment commander. His wife works at the embassy in Ireland and is a former Marine lieutenant. She joined the Corps because she noticed that "Marines love their jobs, and all I ever wanted was to love my work, so I became a Marine."

SSgt Piazza said, "This is a great chance to learn the field administration side of being a staff NCO."

The U.S. State Department has had a long and special relationship with the Marine Corps. The Marine Corps Embassy Security Group (MCESG) headquarters is located aboard Marine Corps Base Quantico, Va. It is a unique command: one that rivals some of the world's most prominent multinational corporations. The commanding officer, much like a CEO, has a daunting worldwide task.

His area of operations spans 18 time zones in 133 countries with detachments of Marine security guards standing post in 148 locations.

With nine regional commands located in five countries around the world, Col Vince Cruz's command has a mission that many other leaders would consider extremely challenging, to include operation of one of the most prestigious schools in the U.S. Marine Corps.

The social event of the year is always the Marine Birthday Ball, and, with a few good Marines, perfection is sought and found in rehearsal after rehearsal—followed by more rehearsal.

Standards are high, and training is rigorous. The Marines selected for the Marine security guard program must have a personal and professional history that can stand the scrutiny required for a high-level security clearance. These Marines attend a six-week school. Their training includes security protocol, defensive tactics and weapons training, as well as an awareness of an embassy lifestyle, social etiquette and a country's local customs.

The qualified Marines, who complete this physically and mentally demanding school, spend the following three years at various posts around the globe. Some may be hardship posts and more austere than others, but all have the risks of danger and terrorist threats.

The days of the architecturally splendid embassies are history; the current security environment demands new and more complex State Department facilities, which are designed to meet the ever-changing force-protection standards. Ask our U.S. Embassy in Dublin's Regional Security Officer (RSO), Michael

Rohlfs. He shows respect for Marines by stating with all sincerity: "Marine security guards are the steel spine of every embassy's security program. As individuals, Marine security guards serve as ambassadors, on both a professional and social level, to each country in which they are assigned and continue to do so with professionalism and honor."

The mission for protecting embassies around the world is growing and so is the Marine headquarters tasked with providing trained Marines to U.S. embassies. A new MSG Training Center will have facilities modeled after a real embassy. The Training Center will replicate the environment the Marines will experience and defend when they stand watch at the traditional Post One in a place far from home.

Perhaps now you "get it," and you understand je ne sais quoi, that mysterious quality. Indeed, it is our splendid American Marines who embody the French phrase. When weary and stressed U.S. citizens who are troubled in a faraway clime and place arrive at our embassy or consulate, their first sight will be a welcomed one. It will be a disciplined warrior—a diplomat attired in dress blues and standing tall at Post One.

Author's note: A heartfelt fair winds to the late Col John Ripley, who made his last journey to Ireland to speak at the MSG mess night in Limerick and inspired this story, as well as to Col Vince Cruz and his MSG leathernecks, who motivate all who meet them.

Editor's note: Patrick "P.T." Brent, an infantry Marine, served with 2/24 and as a UPI military correspondent, embedded in Afghanistan, Iraq and Africa.

*See first to understand,
then to be understood.*

Stephen Covey

Defense Language Institute
The Tower of Babel Versus Modern Warfare
By P.T. Brent

Long before there was our Corps of Marines, there were biblical accounts of the "Tower of Babel" located in a city that united all humanity, all speaking the same language. Because this tower was built to honor man and not the Almighty, God struck it down and changed our world order forever. Each and every tribe was given a different language, causing communication obstacles and perhaps thus creating an interesting perspective on the need for the Defense Language Institute in Monterey, Calif.

Combat has changed during the centuries, but the need for intelligence is a constant. Understanding cultures and languages helps provide that intelligence and gain the combat edge. In today's combat environment, in Operations Iraqi Freedom and Enduring Freedom, a Marine may be helping to build a new school and passing out treats to local children, then, a few seconds later, might be hunkering down to take out a sniper or a vehicle-borne improvised explosive device. Skills inherent in fighting and winning in this type war are unique.

Language has become an essential

Above: This 2007 DLI command photograph reflects the multiservice diversity of the student body and the military-civilian staff that supports the thousands of students who come through the institute each year. (Photo courtesy of Presidio of Monterey Public Affairs Office)

Inset: A great deal of the studying can be done via computer and in the barracks as demonstrated by PFC Andrew J. Ross, who is working to perfect Arabic skills.

part of winning the global war on terrorism. Marines and personnel from all military branches must have an understanding of the culture and the languages of the people who live in the deployment area. Clearly, one of the Corps' missions is to assist the indigenous people of the various countries in their quests for a better way of life. That continuing need for language and cultural understanding reinforces the importance of the

Defense Language Institute.

Marine Staff Sergeant Steve Dixon from Fitzgerald, Ga., realized the vital need for understanding language even before entering DLI. Months earlier, SSgt Dixon was standing guard at a checkpoint in Iraq when a local family approached the Marines.

The family members were suffering from serious wounds caused by an IED. Dixon's rudimentary Arabic skills were key to maintaining calm in

This aerial view provides a perspective on the institute's Presidio of Monterey facilities and the scenic majesty of surrounding countryside.

a tense situation. When organizing Marines to escort the wounded children and parents to the hospital in Ramadi, Dixon's knowledge of Arabic helped the family survive.

SSgt Dixon later used his Arabic in helping train Iraqi soldiers to take on the fight against the insurgents. He is attending DLI to hone his Arabic skills so that he can continue to make a difference when serving in the global war on terrorism.

One of the World's Best Language Schools

The Defense Department's remarkable language school was founded during November 1941 in an old airplane hangar at San Francisco's Crissy Field. It began as a top-secret school for teaching Japanese language in preparation for World War II. The honor and heroism of these original students is depicted in the institute's "Yankee Samurai" exhibit.

The school has grown in size and importance since then, and now DLI offers 24 basic language courses at the Presidio of Monterey. All branches of the military quarter their students in this unique joint training atmosphere.

There currently are 292 Marine students at DLI—part of a Department of Defense student body of 3,500 taught by a faculty of 1,700 of which 98 percent are native to the language in which they teach. The average class has six students or less. The course packages range in duration from 12 to 63 weeks. DLI is fully accredited, and

Monterey Bay, Calif.

Commodore John Drake Sloat's sailors and Marines landed to claim the Monterey Bay area for the United States 7 July 1846. According to the September 1926 "Leatherneck" article, "The American Flag Hoisted at Monterey, California, July 7, 1846" by E. N. McClellan, the flag went up "...never to come down. About one hundred sixty-five Bluejackets and eighty-five Marines were landed on that date. The Marine officers present were Captain Ward Marston and Second Lieutenant Henry W. Queen, both of the 'Savannah' and Lieutenant W.A.T. Maddox of the 'Cyane.' Orderly Sergeant John McCabe was in charge of the 'Levant's' Marine Guard that was included in the landing party."

The Marines hoisted the Stars and Stripes as part of the "Manifest Destiny" push to expand U.S. borders from sea to shining sea. While Defense Language Institute Marines share the common heritage of all Marines and that of those leathernecks off Commodore Sloat's warships, they also carry on the same traditions our Corps has had for more than two centuries—they know they are a part of a disciplined force well trained for the global war on terrorism.

The Presidio commands spectacular views of Monterey Bay. The area is a year-round tourist mecca with Carmel-by-the-Sea located right next door. Downtown Monterey and its shops, restaurants and beaches are an easy walk from the Presidio. It is a high-security, closed post with tightly controlled access. A perfect setting for dedicated warriors to learn their craft while also enjoying their surroundings. —P.T. Brent

based on an agreement with nearby Monterey Peninsula College, students may earn an Associate of Arts degree directly from the institute. By the way, spouses are permitted to take courses at DLI too—without charge.

The DLI curriculum is fast-paced: Each student reads about a textbook per week. Corporal Ben Walker, a Texan and a summa cum laude graduate in linguistics from Houston's Rice University, said: "They throw a great deal on you at once. Study after hours is critical; vocabulary has to be learned on your own. After four college years of learning linguistics—this is one tough program."

Walker is enrolled in the challenging 63-week Chinese course. While required to meet the class schedule and continue satisfactory progress toward graduation, he and other DLI students also are encouraged to become involved in community service projects. The DLI students average 75,000 hours of volunteer service each year.

Although the DLI schedule is daunting, top-notch facilities go a long way to ameliorating the task at hand, which is to gain fluency in the designated language while learning the cultures associated with language. Ninety percent of the students live in well-appointed residence halls. DLI's Hobson Student Center also has state-of-the-art recreation facilities.

Newly promoted Sergeant Heather Hill, a DLI student and mother of two, takes her children with her to DLI each day and places them in the day-care center while she studies Arabic and prepares for later deployment to the operating forces. One of the world's-finest language schools, DLI also provides family support services and opportunities.

Cutting-edge technology and instruction are assured by a well-funded DLI budget. The institute has more than 500 classrooms, 1,200 language lab terminals, 17 permanent dormitories and two dining facilities. There are 4,607 portable digital language devices (iPods), 1,900 notebook computers that are issued to students, and more than 600 "smart boards," which make DLI the quintessential center for language and cultural learning.

For deployed Marines, DLI produces language survival kits in 36 languages. The kit consists of a pocket-size book and a CD, which will orient the field Marine to 10 different topics from civil affairs to medicine. These are available through the Web site: www.LingNet.org.

LingNet hosts the institute's "Countries in Perspective" informational series and the Global Language Online Support System (GLOSS). LingNet also provides a quick portal for access to additional educational material produced and made available by DOD and other government agencies and departments.

"The young men and women who pass through the halls of the Marine Detachment at DLI are literally the sensing organs for the entire organism engaged in the GWOT and long war.

One of the pleasures of command is recognizing excellence through promotions. On the left, LCpl Ben Walker becomes a corporal and, on the right, Cpl Heather Hill becomes a sergeant.

Their skills separate the wheat from the chaff and provide substance and solidity to what would otherwise only be guessed at or missed. They are the conduit for commanders to know not just the words spoken, but the meaning and subtle references that would be lost," according to Major James Manel, Commanding Officer, Marine Det.

Master Gunnery Sergeant Joe Brearley at DLI's Marine barracks reminds his Marines when they report aboard: "You are Marines first and students second, and never forget, while here in school you are still rock-hard members of the world's finest gun club."

Editor's note: P.T. Brent is an infantry Marine veteran. He has served with 2/24 and as a UPI military correspondent embedded with U.S. Armed Forces in Afghanistan, Iraq and Africa. He currently resides in Honolulu.

The following story was reprinted with the kind permission of its original publisher, "Leatherneck Magazine, the Magazine of the Marines," published by the Marine Corps Association, Quantico, Va.

The Marines I have seen around the world
have the cleanest bodies,
the filthiest minds,
the highest morale,
and the lowest morals of any group
of animals I have ever seen.
Thank God for the
United States Marine Corps!"

Eleanor Roosevelt

30 June 1945

The Kingdom of Denmark
Marines Jump at Chance to Serve In the Shadow of Vikings
By P.T. Brent

"I am proud of the young men in Embassy Copenhagen's Marine Security Guard Detachment. It's not just a question of feeling more secure with the Marines manning Post 1, which I do, of course. It's what they contribute to our diplomatic mission in a broader sense. They are the first Americans that embassy visitors meet, and they represent our country extremely well. They are the embodiment of American patriotism. They are also an integral part of our internal embassy community."
—James P. Cain
U.S. Ambassador to Denmark

What a deal ... being an MSG—a Marine security guard—based at the American Embassy in Copenhagen, Denmark.

"The art of diplomacy is telling your family and friends you are being sent away to embassy duty in Scandinavia and not grinning," said one veteran Marine officer. What a chance to see the world, experience

The architecturally distinctive Copenhagen city hall serves to remind leathernecks in the American Embassy Marine Security Guard Detachment that they have a unique opportunity to serve their country and Corps while experiencing a different culture and learning a new language.

different cultures and people, learn languages and have a unique job that really counts.

Marine security guards are all volunteers. They are outstanding Marines chosen from the best the Corps has to offer. Mature young Americans, on the average, they have completed one tour in the Marine Corps prior to this handpicked State Department duty. Unmarried, except for the detachment commander, and provided security clearances before they become an embassy or consulate watchstander, these Marines are "Ambassadors in Blue."

For many, this is a pivotal moment. It is the duty assignment that will decide if they will commit to a long-term career as a leatherneck. Not all candidates graduate from the training. Their appearance, civilian attire (paid for by the Marine Corps), maturity and a record of no previous violations all goes into the evaluation during the training at the Marine Security Guard School in Quantico, Va. Each Marine who graduates earns the seal of approval and an assignment as a new "Ambassador in Blue."

In the land of Hans Christian Andersen, Tivoli Gardens, Hamlet and Vikings, everyone appears squared away and content. This is a highly successful social-welfare state, heavily unionized (75 percent of the work force) with no poor or homeless. The government mandates caring for the poor, disabled and elderly. All Danes have 100 percent health-care coverage, underwritten in totality by their taxes.

All levels of education are free,

The Danish military guard at the Amalienborg Palace, the royal residence in Copenhagen, conducts formal changing of the guard ceremonies each day, reinforcing the importance of the representational responsibilities of the military.

including college. It is the law. Unfortunately, there is the "other" news. Danish taxes are highest in the world. From 50 percent to 68 percent of Danes' pay (depending on income) is taxed. They have a high minimum wage, about $2,000 U.S. per month *after* taxes (i.e., $20 U.S. per hour).

The country is energy independent, but its gasoline is priced at $9 a gallon, and the tax on a new or used vehicle is 200 percent. It is no wonder in Copenhagen city that bicycles abound, far outnumbering motor vehicles. Hundreds are parked at train stations and at the city's ubiquitous bike racks. There are safe biking lanes throughout the country. These well-mannered cyclists are of every age group and often very well dressed. They venture out in all weather; peddling through their rugged winters can be tough.

"The Little Mermaid" sculpture, a country landmark in the Copenhagen harbor, was based on a fairy tale by Hans Christian Andersen. It is Denmark's Eiffel Tower and attracts almost one million tourists every year. Edvard Eriksen sculptured her in bronze, using his wife, Eline, as his model.

Sadly, in the last generation she has been vandalized eight times, but lovingly restored to her original splendor by the proud Danes.

"All my Marine pals are jealous, and my civilian friends want to visit me. You know, we Marines are pretty popular with the locals," said a smiling Sergeant Janer "Esco" Escobales, just after coming off duty at Post One in the United States Embassy in the Kingdom of Denmark.

Just before he shoved off for leave with friends in Barcelona, Spain, Escobales related: "Since 9th grade I always wanted to be aMarine." This infantry Marine has received several meritorious promotions and knows that his mom, Maribel, back in Harrisburg, Pa., is quite proud of him.

Sgt Mike Cates is from San Antonio. His uncle, Marine veteran Thomas Massey Boyd, was killed in action in Vietnam. Cates' father was a Marine also, and both father and uncle inspired him to enlist. Currently on his first MSG posting, Sgt Cates said he considers this to be "real duty" after a series of technical jobs.

In three MSG postings, regardless of conditions, Sgt Clement Benloss derived many dividends from each MSG job. The sergeant's No. 1 divi-

MarDet Copenhagen: SSgt N.R. Deitz, SSgt N. Singh, Sgt J. Escobales, Sgt M.W. Cates and Sgt D.L. Swinney. Absent from the photo is Sgt C.S. Benloss.

The Marine Corps Birthday Ball, hosted by the MarDet leathernecks, is the social occasion of the year for the American Embassy.

A symbol of Denmark, the Little Mermaid, approximately four feet high, sits on her rock looking at the water near the cruise ship pier at Langelinie, Copenhagen.

end is clearly his fiancée. He met her during his first MSG an assignment assignment in Brazil. They plan to be married in Copenhagen at the end of his MSG tour and will start their new life at Marine Corps Base Camp Pendleton, Calif. Copenhagen is the sergeant's last MSG post. He also was posted in Bahrain for a year, where he added Arabic to his list of language skills, which includes Portuguese and Danish.

"My dad is a Marine, and my two brothers went into the Corps. I wanted to be a Marine since I was 14," said Sgt David Swinney from Newton, N.C. This proud Irishman added, "I overslept the day of [the college] SAT and knew then I better enlist." He first served in Prague, Czech Republic, and then Kenya, which represented a return to Africa. He was based in Djibouti— the Horn of Africa—earlier in his career. "Some Marines perceive this job as more glamorous than it really is....However, it is a 100 percent worthwhile endeavor," Swinney said.

Staff Sergeant Nick Singh hails from El Paso, Texas, where his family

trains racing horses. "Embassy duty is what you make of it. In Saudi Arabia, I rode the local prince's horses. In India, I got to see the Taj Mahal." This motor transport Marine continued, "These overseas assignments allow you to develop new hobbies and interests."

Denmark is SSgt Singh's third and therefore last post as an MSG Marine. SSgt Singh added that it "beats me why recruiters are not passing the word about embassy duty."

SSgt Nicholas R. Deitz, the detachment commander, has the most challenging and unique job. Raised in Eugene, Ore., he set out to join the U.S. Navy police force and noticed the difference between the Navy recruiters and the Marine recruiters. On the spot, SSgt Deitz decided to seek a change in his life. He related how intense the screening process is for MSG Marines.

The staff sergeant has his family with him on this tour. His wife completed two tours before leaving the Corps to spend more time with the

Ultimate MSG Commitment

The Copenhagen MSG leathernecks have rapidly become a security force their country can and will rely upon; however, while the duty can be awe-inspiring, it can be dangerous. The Marines of the MSG Detachment Copenhagen are cut from the same scarlet-and-gold fabric as the following Marine security guards who made the supreme sacrifice while assigned as MSGs:

Corporal James C. Marshall: Saigon Embassy, 1968
Sergeant Charles W. Turberville: Phnom Penh, Cambodia, 1971
Lance Corporal Darwin D. Judge: Saigon Embassy, 1975
Cpl Charles McMahon Jr.: Saigon Embassy, 1975
Sgt Bobby Romero: Paris Embassy, 1978
Cpl Steven J. Crowley: Pakistan Embassy, 1979
Cpl Robert V. McMaugh: Beirut Embassy, 1983
Staff Sergeant Thomas T. Handwork: El Salvador Embassy, 1985
Sgt Patrick R. Kwiatkowski: El Salvador Embassy, 1985
Sgt Gregory H. Weber: El Salvador Embassy, 1985
SSgt Bobby J. Dickson: El Salvador Embassy, 1985
Sgt Jesse N. Aliganga: Kenya Embassy, 1998

—P.T. Brent

children. Prior to becoming a detachment commander, SSgt Deitz served two tours in Okinawa and three tours in Iraq, as well as one tour with the 13th Marine Expeditionary Unit in Afghanistan in Operation Enduring Freedom.

"We are the only Marines in DK now. The Denmark Marine Corps was transferred into their army, where every qualified Danish male is drafted for mandatory service. The Danish Marine Regiment, in spite of being folded into the Danish army, still keeps some of their seagoing traditions," said SSgt Deitz.

"My Marines demand little, but the State Department offers a Marine House that is quite comfortable with a private workout room and some pretty nice amenities."

Clearly proud of his Marines, Deitz added, "It is an honor and a privilege to be able to serve my country. I joined the Corps to see the world, and that's exactly what I am doing."

Editor's note: P.T. Brent is an infantry Marine veteran. He has served with 2/24 and as a UPI military correspondent embedded with U.S. Armed Forces in Afghanistan, Iraq and Africa. He currently resides in Honolulu.

But somewhere on this globe we call earth, Marines gather and quietly signal to each other, "Happy Birthday, Marine" as they continue their combat assignment.

Major Ralph Stoney Bates, USMC (Ret.)

This story is dedicated to Major Ralph Stoney Bates, USMC (Ret.). Major Bates, is the author of the upcoming books: "Short Rations for the Marines," a nonfiction anthology, and "A Marine Called Gabe: World's Greatest Leatherneck," a biography on General John Archer Lejeune (Luh jern).

Lejeune, Luh jern
And How to Say It

By P.T. Brent

The common denominator of all Marine Corps virtues is "respect." Therefore, it would, indeed, be difficult, if not impossible to find a Marine, past or present, who has earned our respect more than Lieutenant General John Archer Lejeune, pronounced Luh jern. Every year, Marines worldwide read, as ordered in November of 1921, LtGen Lejeune's Birthday Message, which enhances our much-envied 10 Nov. tradition.

The birthday traditions take a distant second place to the fact that the general is credited with single-handedly saving the Corps after World War I. Respect for the general, post

his passing, has reached almost religious proportions. A major base in North Carolina, memorial halls at the U.S. Naval Academy in Annapolis, Md., and Marine Corps Base Quantico, Va., as well as a major highway in Florida have all been named in honor of the general and his impressive military record.

"Respect" is the issue down in Pointe Coupee (pronounced pon kupee) Parish, La., where the citizens, including nearly 200 descendants of the general's family, have for two centuries pronounced the family name

The Louisiana state historical marker tells all who pass that LtGen John A. Lejeune was born in Innis, La., but little remains of the old house. Lejeune descendant Jacques LaCour (right) stands in front of the ruins of the Lejeune home.

"The World's Greatest Marine"

This statue of LtGen John A. Lejeune stands in front of the Pointe Coupee Parish courthouse in New Roads, La. Louisiana businessman Patrick F. Taylor, who like LtGen Lejeune, believed in education, funded this bronze tribute as well as a similar one located in the traffic circle aboard MCB Camp Lejeune, N.C.

Lieutenant General John A. Lejeune would have taken immediate umbrage with the above appellation; however, many Corps historians would have backed that title. In a review of Marine Corps history and the hallmarks that made the 20th century, LtGen Lejeune would be most prominent.

From the beginning, he had to fight to receive a commission in the Corps. Initially, because of his academic standing at the U.S. Naval Academy, he had been assigned to the Engineer Corps. He successfully challenged that decision in order to become a Marine.

He became a decorated combat officer, creative educator and planner, who led the Corps in expeditionary preparations. His leadership gave the Corps the Fleet Marine Force, precursor to today's operating forces. It was in the passageways of Congress where he made sure the Corps had tenure and status. He founded The Marine Corps Association at Guantanamo Bay, Cuba, in 1913.

His World War I record, including command of the 2nd Division in combat, and decorations speak for themselves. He retired as a major general on 10 Nov. 1929 and was advanced to the rank of lieutenant general on the retired list in February 1942.

Surely, there is room in Marine lexicon for the correct use of the general's name.

—P.T. Brent

Luh jern, albeit spelled Lejeune. Today's Lejeune family traces its heritage back to the Jean Baptiste Lejeune family. Louisiana is "gyrene" territory, with six Marine generals hailing from the bayous, including two Commandants, Major General Commandant John Lejeune, the 13th, and General Robert H. Barrow, the 27th.

Family members share the story in a kind and gentle fashion, that when Northerners (aka Yankees) say the name, they change it without regard for the correct pronunciation. In our lastest generation of leathernecks, many have lost the correct sound for the name Lejeune.

The Lejeune name is a legacy in this southern parish where the general was born on 10 Jan. 1867. The French heritage, Cajun and Creole accents, and the Napoleonic legal codes all blend to create a chivalrous way of life in southern Louisiana.

LtGen Lejeune's descendants such as Jacques LaCour, whose family owns the Old Hickory Plantation where John Lejeune was born, as well as the parish administrator, Owen J. "Jimmy" Bello, and the parish historian would like to know how their most famous son's name became so widely misspoken. In the 1960s and '70s, consensus has it that at least half the Marines used the correct LeJERN articulation. Time and inattention in other climes has diminished the proper pronunciation of the general's name.

There is absolute unanimity on the correct pronunciation at his birthplace. One retired Marine told me: "It was like tomato/tomato." He later recanted

and assured me that leathernecks pronouncing "LeJERN" are both on target as well as respectful. So where did it go awry?

It took several generations and some notable sea stories to have our illustrious leatherneck's name so mispronounced.

One Marine major's French lady tried convincing her Marine that the French pronounce the name Luh Joon, which means "the young." Clearly, she had not been to Pointe Coupee, La., and learned of the Lejeune (Luh jern) family legacy.

Brian Costello, noted Pointe Coupee historian and the author of "The House of Lejeune," plus 17 other books on this charming area of the old South stated: "When we hear Camp Lejeune mispronounced on the television, we cringe!"

Jimmy Bello added, "General Lejeune is the most prominent gentleman this parish has ever raised. We all wish and hope his name will be respected and said correctly. We are in phase one of creating a Lejeune History Center for visitors to Pointe Coupee."

"My dad, a decorated Marine who fought at Iwo Jima, always insisted our family and others pronounce the general's name properly," Jacques LaCour said. "Our recent generation has slacked off on this respect."

A humorous instance of Marines and names was related by the keynote speaker at the 10 Nov. 2006 dedication ceremony for the National Museum of the Marine Corps in Triangle, Va.

Jim Lehrer, the prominent National

LtGen Lejeune's Birthday Message

(Marine Corps Order No. 47 (Series 1921),
Headquarters, U.S. Marine Corps, Washington, 1 Nov. 1921)

759. The following will be read to the command on the 10th of November, 1921, and hereafter on the 10th of November of every year. Should the order not be received by the 10th of November, 1921, it will be read upon receipt.

(1) On November 10, 1775, a Corps of Marines was created by a resolution of Continental Congress. Since that date many thousand men have borne the name "Marine." In memory of them it is fitting that we who are Marines should commemorate the birthday of our corps by calling to mind the glories of its long and illustrious history.

(2) The record of our corps is one which will bear comparison with that of the most famous military organizations in the world's history. During 90 of the 146 years of its existence[,] the Marine Corps has been in action against the Nation's foes. From the Battle of Trenton to the Argonne, Marines have won foremost honors in war, and [in] the long eras of tranquility at home, generation after generation of Marines have grown gray in war in both hemispheres and in every corner of the seven seas, that our country and its citizens might enjoy peace and security.

(3) In every battle and skirmish since the birth of our corps, Marines have acquitted themselves with the greatest distinction, winning new honors on each occasion until the term "Marine" has come to signify all that is highest in military efficiency and soldierly virtue.

(4) This high name of distinction and soldierly repute we who are Marines today have received from those who preceded us in the corps. With it we have also received from them the eternal spirit which has animated our corps from generation to generation and has been the distinguishing mark of the Marines in every age. So long as that spirit continues to flourish[,] Marines will be found equal to every emergency in the future as they have been in the past, and the men of our Nation will regard us as worthy successors to the long line of illustrious men who have served as "Soldiers of the Sea" since the founding of the corps.

JOHN A. LEJEUNE
Major General Commandant

Above: On Nov. 10, 2007, 2dLt Learlin Lejeune III, Weapons Platoon leader, Company B, 1st Battalion, Ninth Marine Regiment, Second Marine Division, reads the traditional Marine Corps Birthday message as directed by his great-great uncle, John A. Lejeune.
Below: Second Lt Lejeune, an Acadia Parish, La., native (left), continues a family tradition of Marine service.

Public TV journalist and news anchor for the "The News Hour With Jim Lehrer," told the audience about his arrival at the train station on the Quantico base for basic officer training. (See Leatherneck, May 2007, for Lehrer interview.)

"The DI told us to answer up, 'Here, sir!' when our name was called, and he got to mine, and he said, 'Le-here-er-er.'

And, like some kind of idiot, I blurted out, 'It's pronounced Lehrer, sir!' "

Lehrer went on to note that he then heard the terrifying click, click, click of the leather heels on the wooden deck of the station made by the drill instructor, who marched down and placed his face an inch from the new officer candidate, as he loudly and clearly said: "Candidate, if I say your name is Little Bo Peep, your name is Little Bo Peep!"

That story, now paraphrased and cleaned up a bit, is the way the future Second Lieutenant Lehrer gained a new name.

A few months ago a Lejeune descendant, who is now 2dLt Learlin Lejeune, pronounced Lur lin LeJERN, an infantry officer, arrived at Quantico. He, too, decided wisely to flow with the misuse of his legendary name rather than correct the non-commissioned officer in charge.

Likewise, now-Corporal Jean Lejeune arrived at Marine Corps Recruit Depot Parris Island, S.C., for recruit training and his junior DI demonstrated little interest in bonding with the new recruit by correctly calling him LeJERN. Later, when his brother Shane Lejeune enlisted—he is now serving in Fallujah—he experienced the same communication challenge. Perhaps educating your senior NCOs upon arrival in the Marine Corps is not the wisest way to strike up a close and intimate rapport

Welcome Home

...to the most sharply disciplined and aggressive fighting force the world has ever known!

and Marines...say & speak my name correctly: Luh-JERN.

Semper Fi!

ILLUSTRATION BY MIKE DAVIS

This billboard pronunciation guide, sponsored by the author, greets those traveling on roadways near MCB Camp Lejeune.

with them.

Etymology, the study of the word origins and their usage, offers some interesting comparisons. In English, there are invisible "Rs," i.e., when General Lejeune was Colonel Lejeune, there was an "R" sound in both names—Kernel LeJERN. Dr. Thomas Klingler, associate professor and chair of the French and Italian

Department, Tulane University, New Orleans, did research for his doctoral dissertation at Pointe Coupee where he worked on a Creole-French dictionary.

On the pronunciation of the Lejeune name, Professor Klingler believes one hypothesis may be that many non-French speaking people had trouble with the "Luh Zhun" sound and over time inserted into common usage the "R" sound, i.e., "Je" has been used as "JER" in southern Louisiana. The Pointe Coupee accents are a mélange of French vocabulary and African grammar.

Marines treasure and respect their history and traditions. The Lejeune family believes that, in time, the general's name will be put back on track.

The Battle of Guadalcanal, in 1942, may not have been a Marine fight had not the 13th Commandant pursued amphibious warfare with a passion. Our Marines may have been limited to Navy police details, and the Fleet Marine Force may have never existed. On the Corps' Birthday on the 'Canal, the First Marine Division paused to recognize the general's treasured tradition. A few short days later on 20 Nov. 1942, John Archer Lejeune, 75, died and was buried with honors at Virginia's Arlington National Cemetery.

John Archer Lejeune (LeJERN) raised the bar in our Corps from the time he entered the U.S. Naval Academy, graduating in the Class of 1888, to his leadership in World War I and his fight to keep our Corps of Marines prominent in the War Department's long-term planning. The rock-hard fact is: We Marines owe our 13th Commandant our honor, courage, commitment and above all RESPECT.

Author's note: A heartfelt Semper Fi to the Lejeune family and the chivalrous and gentile people of Pointe Coupee Parish, La.

Editor's note: Patrick "P.T." Brent is an infantry Marine who served with 2/24. He has been a UPI correspondent, embedded with U.S. military units in Afghanistan, Iraq and Africa. A Honolulu businessman, he is a "founder" for the National Museum of the Marine Corps near Quantico and The Marine Memorial at Pearl Harbor.

A ship without Marines is like a garment without buttons.

Admiral David D. Porter

The Pride of the Pacific
The 11th Marine Expeditionary Unit
Storms the Golden Gate During Fleet Week

By P.T. Brent

Flash back to a legendary moment in 1946: World War II has ended and Marines are celebrating at the famous Top of the Mark restaurant and lounge on San Francisco's Nob Hill . . .

On Oct. 7, 2010, leathernecks from the 11th Marine Expeditionary Unit performed a live "rerun," standing at attention and singing "The Marines' Hymn" with orchestral accompaniment. The room rocked with the resounding approval of the guests; love of country and Corps reigned at the top of Nob Hill.

Fleet Week San Francisco was a time for displaying the Navy-Marine team at its finest—Inset: Sgt Justin L. Gerdes, an 11th MEU explosive ordnance disposal technician, set up an exhibit that included a bomb disposal robot.

Below: Professional photographer Christopher Michel entered San Francisco harbor for Fleet Week on board USS *Makin Island*, capturing this dramatic photograph. More of his photographs are available at www.christophermichel.com.

Bay was
~~~~~~~

Above: The 1stMarDiv Band "wowed" everyone with performances all over San Francisco.
Left: Retired MajGen J. Michael "Mike" Myatt (foreground), president and CEO of the Marines' Memorial Club & Hotel, was a driving force in ensuring the success of Fleet Week San Francisco.

The day before, the 11th MEU, on board USS Makin Island (LHD-8), sailed beneath the Golden Gate Bridge with Marines and sailors manning the rail in their dress uniforms. What a sight and what a welcome! A fireboat launching geysers of water was only the beginning of the red carpet treatment offered the fleet by arguably America's most picturesque city.

This was the most anticipated liberty call of the year. Perfect fall weather blessed the Italian festival, the concerts by the First Marine Division Band and a performance by the "Blue Angels." The U.S. Navy's world-renowned flight demonstration squadron screamed over and under the Golden Gate and pivoted around Alcatraz and Telegraph Hill. All events were viewed and applauded by thousands, including Senator Dianne Feinstein and George Shultz—a World War II Marine veteran and former secretary of state under President Ronald Reagan.

Scene after memorable scene was celebrated by the 1,500 sailors and Marines while on five days of liberty. Many of those scenes were punctuated by magic moments straight out of Hollywood classics like "On the Town" and "Anchors Aweigh."

Residents and tourists alike treasured the Marines and sailors. Each night, there were countless new stories for them to share upon returning to *Makin Island*, guided missile frigate USS *Curts* (FFG-38), guided missile destroyer USS *Pinckney* (DDG-91), and mine countermeasures ships USS *Pioneer* (MCM-9) and USS *Chief* (MCM-14), docked in the heart of San Francisco. Also on hand were Coast Guard cutters and ships from the Canadian navy, which is celebrating its 100th anniversary.

The revitalized Fleet Week, Oct. 7-12, was a smashing success. Under the leadership of Major General J. Michael "Mike" Myatt, USMC (Ret), president and CEO of the Marines' Memorial Club & Hotel, a Navy-Marine team expertly organized the event in the city one journalist dubbed, "Baghdad by the Bay."

Gung-ho

Rarely has a ship been more aptly chosen for Fleet Week in San Francisco. The last time a ship bearing the name "*Makin Island*" entered the San Francisco Bay was Nov. 5, 1945, when the aircraft carrier USS *Makin Island* (CVE-93) returned from WWII. Both ships honor the gungho spirit of the Marines who raided Butaritari Island, Makin Atoll in August 1942. Lieutenant Colonel Evans F. Carlson, who commanded the 2d Marine Raider Battalion in the attack on Makin, coined the term "gung-ho" after his experiences with the Chinese field army.

The word "gung-ho," originating from the Chinese word for "working together in harmony," and the spirit of the word have rapidly become a part of leatherneck lore, and that spirit was definitely evident in Fleet Week.

The new USS *Makin Island* (LHD-8) is the largest amphibious assault ship in the Navy, second in size only to a carrier; she also is the last of the Wasp-class LHDs to be commissioned. Christened Aug. 19, 2006, she was sponsored by Mrs. Silke Hagee, wife of General Michael Hagee, 33rd Commandant of the Marine Corps, and launched on Sept. 15, 2006.

The ship's capabilities would surely mystify LtCol Carlson's Marine Raiders. *Makin Island* has a revolutionary propulsion system, which combines gas turbines with an electric drive system, an arrangement similar to the one found in new hybrid cars. As a result, *Makin Island* can travel long distances on comparatively little fuel, an attribute that will save an estimated $250 million in fuel costs over the ship's 40-year life span.

One of Fleet Week's major themes was the power of ships like *Makin Island*—with her prodigious medical capacity, fresh water production facilities, as well as trained personnel—to offer much needed help during a humanitarian crisis. Deep beneath San Francisco, the fault lines are locked, loaded and ready to rock the populace. Clearly, it is not a matter of if a severe quake will strike the city, but when.

Thus, the focus of Fleet Week was on how the military can contribute in the aftermath of a disaster. The military has a long history of furnishing aid to San Francisco; in 1906, USS *Chicago* evacuated 20,000 people from a horrific fire brought on by a major earthquake. When "the big one" hits, the city—surrounded by water on three sides—will have helping hands come from the sea.

"We'll be demonstrating, on the Marina Green [a large park area], desalinization techniques, disaster relief workshops and a working field hospital," said MajGen Myatt, chairman of Fleet Week 2010. "When, not if, a catastrophic earthquake hits San Francisco, we know how to swiftly incorporate the military into humanitarian assistance efforts."

"*Makin Island* has enough beds to house hundreds of displaced citizens and provide rapid medical care," said senior medical officer Lieutenant Commander Adolfo Granados.

"With medical capabilities second only to the U.S. hospital ships USNS *Mercy* and USNS *Comfort*, *Makin Island* has the facilities to deal with mass-casualty situations. Equipped with six operating rooms, a 17-bed ICU, a 50-bed recovery room, a blood bank and digital X-ray machines, *Makin Island* and [her] embarked surgical team can deal with almost any medical emergency, ranging from delivering a child to caring for internal injuries requiring surgery."

In addition to her medical facilities, *Makin Island*'s four reverse osmosis units have the capability to produce up to 200,000 gallons of fresh water per day. The ship can transport this water in bladders via helicopter or amphibious landing craft directly to a crisis zone. Whatever the needs of the mission—the need to provide humanitarian relief or the need to inject combat Marines into a foreign clime without invitation—the wherewithal of *Makin Island* to exert American power overseas is second to none.

Under the command of Colonel Michael R. Hudson, the 11th MEU, embarked in *Makin Island*, is ready for any challenge. The 11th MEU has earned the appellation "The Pride of the Pacific." *Makin Island*'s amphibious versatility, her weaponry, and, above all, her crew and embarked Marines constitute a force of which America can be proud.

The commodore of Amphibious Squadron Five, Captain Burt Quintanilla, USN, might have made a pretty fair "gyrene." Two weeks prior to Fleet Week, CAPT Quintanilla joined the 11th MEU for a grueling hike at Marine Corps Base Camp Pendleton, Calif. He told Gunnery Sergeant Scott Dunn: "The tensile strength of the blue-green partnership

Top: San Franciscans lined the beach to see USS *Makin* enter the harbor and watch the Marines go ashore.

Above left: While on board *Makin Island*, Marines cleaned weapons and readied uniforms to prepare for Fleet Week.

Above right: Of course life aboard ship has its responsibilities and someone has to be the noncommissioned officer in charge of the scullery—LCpl Charlie Roberts didn't mind as he did get liberty call while in port.

Bottom Right: Embarked Marines found *Makin Island*'s living quarters very comfortable.

The Golden Gate

Since its completion in 1937, the Golden Gate Bridge has been the first sight of America for many returning warriors. After four bloody years in the Pacific, thousands of World War II leathernecks returned home to San Francisco's Treasure Island for reassignment or discharge. Some returned to those shores on board the original USS *Makin Island* (CVE-93) in November 1945; they cruised by Alcatraz where, in the spring of 1946, Marine veterans of the Pacific would quell a convict riot.

Now called the Battle of Alcatraz, two platoons of Marines, using tactics that had been designed to flush the Japanese out of pillboxes, drove the convicts into a position that forced their surrender.

Long before the bridge was built by Joseph Strauss, a Chicago engineer, even before the discovery of gold in California, John C. Frémont, with great prescience, dubbed the strait the "Golden Gate." For the '49ers seeking unbridled wealth in the gold fields a few years hence, the name could not have been more appropriate. Driven by greed, sailors abandoned their ships to rot and burn in San Francisco harbor.

During Fleet Week, the Golden Gate welcomed Marines and sailors into one of the world's most beautiful natural harbors, a harbor which was once the optimum location for United States Marine Corps and naval forces. The military presence in San Francisco has diminished over the years. Although the city is famous for antiwar protests, Wilkes Bashford, a prominent San Franciscan, stated, "San Francisco has an unearned reputation for being insensitive to our veterans. On the contrary, while we don't like war, we are extremely supportive of the men and women who have fought for our freedom."

This awesome Fleet Week, which no doubt bolstered the relationship between San Francisco and the military, will hopefully lead to an increased appreciation of our sailors and Marines.

—P.T. Brent

is integral to combat success. The Navy-Marine team continues to win America's wars, one lift, one battle and one crisis at a time."

This team—America's Navy and Marines ready to forward deploy—is ready 24/7 to tackle new missions. The blue-green partnership, exemplified by Fleet Week 2010, strengthens our military by building camaraderie.

Lance Corporal Charlie Roberts, 2nd Battalion, Seventh Marine Regiment, a mortarman from Halton City, Texas, spent the cruise working the scullery alongside sailors. In that spirit, Private First Class Damion Prado recovered money lost by a Marine and spent two days diligently locating the owner.

The MEU's operations officer, LtCol Thomas Prentice, reflected,

It was a memorable occasion for all hands, from manning the rail on the way in—as LtCol Tom Prentice, Ops Officer, 11th MEU, and SgtMaj Derek D. Leggett, Sergeant Major, HMM-364, are doing—to the very last farewell to San Francisco.

"The *Makin Island* 11th MEU/ARG [amphibious ready group] team has the capability to successfully execute any assigned mission at any time and any place on the globe." The second night ashore, the MEU's hardworking operations section, which successfully handles the myriad of detail that goes with an undertaking of this dimension, was hosted by its boss at an uproarious Italian eatery. At the end of dinner, the Marines sang all three verses of "The Marines' Hymn" to an appreciative restaurant crowd.

The 11th MEU is a quick-reaction task force consisting of 2,200 Marines and sailors and is one of three MEUs based on the West Coast. The commanding officer, Col Hudson, has now served with all three of these MEUs: 11th, 13th and 15th.

Asked to comment on his command and the San Francisco deployment, Col Hudson stated: "Golden Gate Fleet Week is an opportunity to display the blue-green team coming from the sea—America's 911 force capable of command and control anywhere on the globe."

Hearts were left in San Francisco as a dynamite liberty call and a Marine-Navy weekend ended to never be forgotten. Fair Winds to "The Pride of the Pacific."

Author's note: Mahalo nui loa (thank you), Lieutenant Justin Smith, as well as the 11th MEU PAOs, who unstintingly worked to make this Fleet Week unique.

Also, thank you to Ramona Robertson, TSOCP, and Laura and Ben Walker for their encouragement and loyalty.

Editor's note: Patrick "P.T." Brent, a frequent Leatherneck contributor, is proud to have been an infantry Marine who served in 2/24. Brent also was a UPI military correspondent, embedded in Afghanistan, Iraq and Africa.

We are United States Marines, and for two and a quarter centuries we have defined the standards of courage, esprit, and military prowess.

Gen. James L. Jones, USMC (CMC); 10 November 2000

FEBRUARY 2009

MAGAZINE OF THE MARINES

Leatherneck

www.mca-marines.org/leatherneck

Marine One
Presidents and Popes Fly With the Best

Getlin's Corner, RVN:
1 MOH, 4 Navy Crosses,
A Pack of Purple Hearts

Combat Leadership—
Instructors Make A
Difference Every Day

"Taking Chance"—A Film
About a Marine's Final Journey

Leatherneck—On the Web
Find More News, Photos and Video on Our Web Site at: www.
mca-marines.org/leatherneck

UNITED STATES OF AMERICA

"Marine One" – Welcome Aboard

By P.T. Brent

IMAGINE: You are on board "Marine One," passing over the nation's capital a mere 200 feet above the ground, on a short final approach to the south lawn of the White House. The Washington Monument, at 555 feet, towers over you. The people below are waving. You have clearance to enter one of the most highly restricted airspaces in the world.

You are on board one of the most storied and historic helicopters, either the venerable Sikorsky VH-3D or the Sikorsky VH-60N. Your helicopter's all-weather capability ensures that the nation's Commander in Chief will be assured safe and timely transport to and from landing zones and locations

COURTESY OF LTCOL GLEN BUTLER

HMX-1 support of the President began when President Eisenhower (seated in this 1957 photo) needed a safe and responsive means of short-range transportation.

President George W. Bush boards Marine One, piloted by the squadron commander, Col Ray "Frenchy" L'Heureux, and Maj Jeremy Deveau, in a lift from Kennebunkport, Maine, to Portsmouth, N.H., in this July 3, 2007, photo. The crew chief is SSgt Timothy Smith, and the security guard is LCpl James Anderson.

that otherwise might take hours in which to drive. Best of all, your trip is completed in comfort and with a communications capability comparable to that of the Oval Office.

It all started in 1957 at President Dwight David "Ike" Eisenhower's summer home on Aquidneck Island, R.I., which is the home of the Naval War College. Ike needed to return to the White House quickly. Typically, for President Eisenhower the trek back to Washington, D.C., required an hour-long ferry ride followed by a 45-minute flight to Andrews Air Force Base, Md., and a 30-minute motorcade to the White House. What a commute!

Clearly, there was a necessity to create a faster way to return to the White House. "Air Force One" was stationed at Andrews Air Force Base, but that big jet just wasn't suited for close trips. President Eisenhower instructed his staff to find a more expeditious way to link up with Air Force One.

Top Accolades for "Marine One" from the Commander in Chief

"I have had some wonderful experiences on 'Marine One'; it is a smooth riding 'bird.' ... There is no doubt in my mind that I am flying with the best our country has to offer."

—George W. Bush

A Marine Helicopter Squadron One (HMX-1) UH-34 Seahorse helicopter was stationed near Aquidneck Island at Naval Air Station Quonset Point, R.I., in case of an emergency. It could be used to fly the President to his awaiting aircraft. President Eisenhower approved the idea, and after the brief seven-minute inaugural flight, the future of Marine One became preordained.

Immediately after the first flight, a naval aide to the President asked HMX-1 personnel to evaluate the south lawn of the White House as a helicopter landing zone. Preliminary assessment and trial flights concluded that ample room was present for a safe landing and departure. The protocols were established, and once again, the United States Marines had landed, this time in the backyard at 1600 Pennsylvania Ave.

According to the current commanding officer of HMX-1, Colonel Raymond F. L'Heureux (la-rué), "Today, HMX-1 has operated in 32 foreign countries. We are globally scrutinized 24/7, every day, and all we do reflects on our squadron, the Marine Corps at large, the White House and, ultimately, the President of the United States. Pride in the mission is the thread that binds our squadron together."

HMX-1's commander distinctly has clarity of command. The mission of Col L'Heureux, call sign "Frenchy," and the squadron under his command is daunting. A 365-day operation, the mission: transporting the leader of the free world. Often with little time to prepare, even for overseas trips, and working with United States Air Force strategic airlift, HMX-1 helicopters have to be positioned in advance to ensure mission success. HMX-1 has strict security not only at its base in Quantico, Va., but wherever it travels. The squadron has a large Marine military police detail operating at the highest levels of security.

The executive versions of the Sikorsky helicopters are unique aircraft, providing the President and his entourage, which often includes cabinet members, press and White House staff, with a comfortable setting. The executive version

COURTESY OF HMX-1

HMX-1 also has provided safe and efficient short-distance transportation to other senior U.S. officials and visiting dignitaries. Maj Kevin Jones and then-Capt Ray "Frenchy" L'Heureux flew Pope John Paul II on his Aug. 12, 1993, visit to World Youth Day in Denver

helicopters are completely carpeted and include pictures on the bulkhead and candy dishes built in for VIP flights. The helicopter radio call sign is, of course, Marine One—when, and only when, the Commander in Chief is on board.

And what an aircraft it is!

Marine One is the most well-engineered, sophisticated and well-maintained helicopter in the world. The aircraft, crew and maintainers overcome the challenges of extreme noise, huge power requirements and heavy vibrations to create and fly a rotary wing aircraft worthy of carrying the President.

Ten years before President Eisenhower's precedent-setting helicopter ride, the year 1947 was a landmark in Corps aviation and tactical doctrine with the basing of HMX-1's first helicopters at what was then Marine Corps Air Station Quantico, Va. HMX-1 performed the first ship-to-shore movement of troops from the deck of an aircraft carrier in an exercise in May 1948. Today, there are more than 700 personnel assigned to the squadron. It is the largest permanently established squadron, and security is paramount.

The sergeant major of the squadron, SgtMaj R.J. Nowak, tells each newly assigned Marine, "Be mindful of who you work for and who you represent—ultimately the White House." These Marines must pass rigid standards; decision-making and initiative are essential qualities. Their job is critical. Everything they do has an effect on our Commander in Chief and, ultimately, our country. SgtMaj

Nowak described them as the "best of the best." The experiences at HMX-1 will serve them well the rest of their lives.

"In the past four months, I have been to every continent, except Antarctica," Staff Sergeant Eric Hernandez said with great pride. This CH-46 Sea Knight mechanic, military occupational specialty 6112, deployed on humanitarian missions to the Philippines and Indonesia before being selected to join this elite squadron. Hernandez now travels with the Marine One team as a crew chief. Their job is to transport the executive helicopters on U.S. Air Force C-17 cargo aircraft to ensure the President's helicopter reaches a location ahead of a presidential visit.

"This is one terrific job; where else could I be in four or five countries and all in just one month," related Sergeant Christopher Johnson, who has been an HMX-1 crew chief since 2007. Johnson had to first complete some rigid screening and training requirements. In accompanying the transport of Marine One aboard a C-17, the sergeant now has traveled to the United Arab Emirates, Egypt, Japan, Germany, Ireland and Korea.

Sergeant Chase Kovarik, a former crew chief, was one of the most photographed Marines in America. "Until the President walks out [of the helicopter after landing], everyone is watching you … not a good time to trip," said Kovarik.

"These are ordinary flights with an exceptional person aboard; they give a Marine a chance to 'polish up.' One fear is to have your cover blow away.

President Signals, "Well Done"

President George W. Bush made a special trip to Marine Corps Air Facility Quantico, Va., Oct. 30, 2008, to express his gratitude for the superb support provided by Marine Helicopter Squadron One throughout his presidency. During his visit to the squadron, he spoke with leathernecks, shaking hands, posing for hundreds of photographs and, in his own style, letting them know on a personal basis that he is aware and appreciates what they endure to support their Commander in Chief. He is the first President to visit HMX-1 at Quantico.

All the gratitude expressed was not one way. The HMX-1 leathernecks had a few unique remembrances for the President. Certainly these are select items that will be conversation pieces for visitors to his Crawford, Texas, ranch, or, in one instance, when he is exercising.

The Marines gathered inside one of the hangars to hear the President speak to all about their performance. Then, it was their turn. First, knowing the President's commitment to physical fitness and his love of mountain and trail biking, he was given a special, aerodynamically efficient, forest green, "Marine One" racing helmet.

Then, in recognition of his many hours on board Marine One watching the rotors turn, he was presented a piece of a Marine One helicopter tail rotor. It was duly noted that this

During President George W. Bush's visit, LCpl John Meekins (above, right) has the honor of presenting him with a unique HMX-1 bicycle racing helmet, and Sgt Michael Kennedy (below, right) presents the President with a Marine One tail rotor section as (from left) Col Ray L'Heureux, squadron CO; LtCol David Braman, XO; and SgtMaj Richard Nowak, squadron sergeant major, look on.

particular item was in excess of needs and his helicopter remained mission ready.

Lastly, the commanding officer, Colonel Raymond F. "Frenchy" L'Heureux, stepped forward to speak for the Marines, noting that it was indeed an honor to be entrusted with the responsibility for supporting the President. Col L'Heureux then presented a special HMX-1 plaque, personalized for President Bush.
—Leatherneck

In this July 4, 2007, photo, Col L'Heureux and Maj Deveau, piloting helicopter NH-1, closest to the Statue of Liberty, and Majors Hal Gibson and Bryan Fanning are en route to MCAF Quantico from Kennebunkport, Maine. (Courtesy of HMX-1)

The answer: stick it on till it hurts and think strong thoughts," said SSgt Hernandez.

These are regular Marines on a special mission. They are part of a living history and have the pride and professionalism to do the job right.

Consider this example: White House representatives contact an HMX-1 crew at home at 0800 on a Sunday. By 1100, work is well underway for a support trip. At 1300, loading onto a C-17 is completed, and the Air Force aircraft takes off for Africa with mid-air refueling. Later, a fresh USAF crew is taken on at a

quick stop in Germany. Then, arriving a few hours later, Marine One is offloaded, test flown and flies into Benin, Africa, and subsequently Ghana, Africa.

All this unique capability comes with a price. Helicopters and plenty of maintenance go hand in hand. Maintenance is intense, and for every hour of flight, HMX-1 maintenance crews need four to six man-hours.

Sometimes labeled "ungainly aerodynamic mavericks," today's helos have earned their stripes. To date, it remains difficult to define the concept of airflow over the rotating wings—aerodynamically the rotor blades provide lift and ultimately allow the aircraft to fly. But HMX-1 air-crews and supporting staff definitely have refined the capability and bring new honors to the Corps and our country with each presidential flight.

Author's note: A book portraying the fabled 60-year history of HMX-1 by LtCol Glen Butler, currently based at MCB Kaneohe Bay, Hawaii, is nearing completion. Butler, a former Marine One pilot, has spent seven years researching and creating a photo-packed historical account worthy of this exceptional squadron. The book will include reminiscences from Presidents, former commanding officers, Commandants and other prominent figures. The Marine Corps History Division has partially funded this endeavor via a research grant, and LtCol Butler will be donating all profits to charities supporting wounded Marines and their families.

Editor's note: Patrick "P.T." Brent is an infantry Marine veteran. He has served with 2/24 and as a UPI military correspondent embedded with U.S. Armed Forces in Afghanistan, Iraq and Africa. He resides in Honolulu.

Marine Helicopter Squadron One was born to test the capabilities of helicopters and grew to even greater responsibilities. Mr. Igor Sikorsky, an early helicopter pioneer seated (wearing a suit) in this 1948 photograph fronting an early HO3S-1 helicopter, visited the squadron on more than one occasion to promote the military benefits of vertical lift.

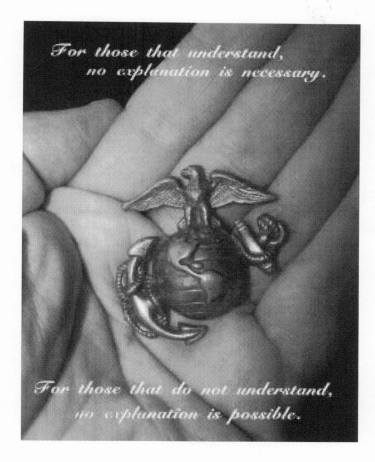

The following story was reprinted with the kind permission of its original publisher, "Leatherneck Magazine, the Magazine of the Marines," published by
the Marine Corps Association, Quantico, Va.

No man or woman is an island.
To exist just for yourself is meaningless.
You can achieve the most satisfaction
when you feel related to some greater
purpose in life, something greater than
yourself.

Denis Waitley

A salute to Steve Petit whose grandma always knew best, so he became a member of the Blue Angels and went to Iwo and Guadalcanal
as the XO of FT1.

One Determined Marine
John Gerber and the Pacific War Museum

Stories and Photos By P.T. Brent

John Vincent Gerber was one of a kind and "the real McCoy." His love of country, Corps and family—wife, Mela, and children—motivated his every effort to build a museum honoring all that he loved. He did that, the "Pacific War Museum."

Y-y-y-y-e-e-e-o-o-w-w, B-A-R-RR-O-O-M! Viet Cong rockets hit near Camp Books' bunkers and shrapnel peppered Marine bunkers. Corporal John Gerber hunkered down praying for another minute of life. It had been a lively week. The prior day, 30 Viet Cong had blocked his Happy Valley convoy. Cpl Gerber had liberty coming and planned to go to Da Nang to hang out with his Guam buddy, Lance Corporal Rufo San Nicholas. San Nicholas was another "homey" who

had enlisted in the Marine Corps with Gerber in June 1969 after graduating from high school in Guam.

LCpl San Nicholas was a firefighter assigned to a Marine aviation unit at Da Nang, Republic of Vietnam. Gerber knew his pal, Rufo, was safe behind the lines, and Da Nang offered good liberty.

Gerber arrived at Da Nang in time to see a somber formation being dismissed. The formation was in honor of San Nicholas, who sacrificed his life trying to save a Marine pilot whose F-4 had been swept by fire and explosions. Gerber was escorted to the morgue to identify the remains of his best friend. It was Sept. 2, 1970, and San Nicholas' remains went home to Guam. He has never been forgotten.

On Memorial Day 1992, Marine veteran John Vincent Gerber and San Nicholas' family attended annual prayers at San Nicholas' gravesite. Gerber recalled that it was an epiphany. He braced, thunderstruck, at the grave of his 19-year-old friend. Gerber made a solemn oath to amend his ways and make his future days, and San Nicholas' death, have meaning. The result, the Pacific War Museum, is a moving story—a tribute to not only

At the grave of his 19-year-old friend, Gerber made a solemn oath to amend his ways and make his future days, and San Nicholas' death, have meaning.

San Nicholas, but all Marines, including Gerber, on the island of Guam.

Guam may seem like a faraway place, but its proximity to areas of significant strategic importance heightens its value to the United States. World War II history is being echoed, as Guam once again is critical to Pacific basin security. Moreover, the pending relocation of 8,000 leathernecks and their families from the Japanese prefecture of Okinawa will bring $15 billion to Guam's economy.

When Marines from Okinawa fly into Guam, they see a giant rooftop sign that reads: "USMC Welcome Back."

Once on land, the Marines will discover that the rooftop belongs to the "best damn leatherneck museum in a 12,000-mile radius." The museum is one motivating saga, which will both dazzle and frustrate other museum authorities worldwide with their multimillion-dollar budgets and staffs. One determined Marine veteran, John Gerber, created this museum with his own hands.

Gerber's lack of financial funding for his museum is more than offset by a plenitude of guts. His charisma, coupled with an intense passion for his mission, made him an unbeatable force as he worked night and day to create a museum based on the Corps' history in Guam.

The Pacific War Museum is located on hallowed ground, Nimitz Hill. Marines from the Third Marine Division battled their way up from Asan Beach to the heights of Fonte Crest during WWII. The Battle of Guam, July 21 to Aug. 10, 1944, was a costly liberation: 1,548 Marines were killed in action and more than 6,000 were wounded.

The museum, located on that crest, is just two clicks (kilometers) from the governor of Guam's headquarters. The Pacific War Museum currently is the only museum in this tropical paradise. It is well planned and executed, honoring all warriors, including three Marine Commandants, who fought to free Guam from the oppressive Japanese. Marine Generals Robert

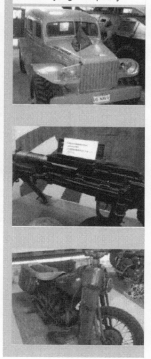

The weapons and vehicles in John Gerber's Pacific War Museum were collected, often in such poor condition that they were almost beyond restoration, and meticulously restored to the very highest quality.

Out of old airport Jetways and cast-off Quonset huts, John Gerber created the "best damn leatherneck museum in a 12,000-mile radius."

Cushman, Lemuel Shepherd and Louis Wilson, a Medal of Honor winner, all served in the invasion. The leathernecks of the 3dMarDiv and the 1st Provisional Marine Brigade, as well as Japanese forces, are honored by the museum.

Clearly, the most memorable place in the museum is the wall where each of the 1,548 KIA Marines is honored. Envision a 10-year effort to acquire this battle site, secure the building materials and commence a passionate search among the rusted detritus of violence. John Gerber often took his own backhoe and excavated the site in search of WWII Japanese and American cannons, bayonets, personal effects, mortars, vehicles and other artifacts. With an indefatigable spirit, he personally restored artifacts to impeccable condition. Seemingly

Marine Corps Drive

"A picture worth a thousand words." Guam's own road warrior, John Gerber, pulled this cart around Guam, some 29 miles, reminding the people of Guam what Marines did for them in World War II and promoting the renaming of Marine Corps Drive. His efforts were successful.

Cruising along Guam's ocean highway is now very special for leathernecks. Road signs marked "Marine Corps Drive" are another example of the spirit of John Vincent Gerber. The original name of "Marine Corps Drive" slowly lost its meaning and impact after World War II. The highway became known as "Marine Drive," meaning a road by the ocean. Ambiguity reigned, and the road no longer was perceived as a Marine Corps highway whose name represented Guam's battlefields of freedom.

There always has been a rare bond between our Corps and the Guamanians. So "Mister Guam," aka "Sergeant" Gerber, decided to return respect to this historic highway. Authorities ignored his attempts at reaffirming the highway's name, not wishing to honor the military accomplishments that motivated the highway name.

After exhausting many appeals, Gerber rigged a carabao-styled cart with one substantial, easily seen sign declaring his goal to rename the highway. He dragged the cart 29 miles between Andersen Air Force Base and the U.S. Naval Base, Guam. Shouts of "Oorah" rang out the entire way from scores of well-wishers, including the governor of Guam, Felix Camacho. This ineluctable Marine finally made his point with the Guamanian legislature. An executive order was written, and the proper signage was placed along Marine Corps Drive.

Modesty, simplicity and honesty made Gerber and his wife, Mela, special. John Gerber was truly "the real McCoy." Gerber, with Mela by his side, worked unstintingly for every patriotic cause imaginable on Guam. His four acre eclectic home overflows with WWII memorabilia such as amtracs and jeeps, as well as one damaged airline Jetway.

Veterans groups and Purple Heart groups met freely at his home's large patio. He supplied a convivial location for their meetings with all the amenities. Marines in the Third Marine Division, using Gerber's equipment, spent more than six weeks trimming 700 palm trees, as well as digging out the weeds and grass, in time for the Marine Battle Color Ceremony at the National Park Service location at Asan Beach in March 2010.

Estimates are that more than 20,000 Marines and other veterans groups have been hosted and fed pro bono by the Gerber family, 3dMarDiv Association and Guam's veterans groups. The local Chamber of Commerce also provides support to the Gerbers and the Pacific War Museum.

Gerber's prodigious work on behalf of veterans was unending. Now it's time for others to step up to keep his legacy, and the legacy of Marines on Guam, alive. I believe they will.

What is that one quality that triumphs over adversity?

Answer: Determination.

And it is spelled J-O-H-N G-E-R-B-E-R.

—P.T. Brent

untouched by time, they now stand as silent sentinels to one of the war's most horrific battles.

Gerber also secured Guam International Airport's old Jetways, which were destroyed in a storm. Imagine these passenger boarding bridges, along with massive steel beams, an elephant Quonset, other Quonsets, major panels of glass from a longtime buddy, scrap steel and donations of cement and pavement from his countless island friends, all combined into one remarkable museum. The museum serves as a platform to educate and entertain Marines as well as men and women of sister services and their veterans and all those who travel to Guam and go to the house that Gerber built.

Historical donations from WWII Marines, sailors and locals arrived and were groomed and placed with historical cards in the museum's two major passageways: one American and the other for Japanese war memorabilia.

For Gerber, the museum was a labor of love. "The U.S. Marines coming to Guam and paying the ultimate sacrifice for our freedom—the meaning of Liberation Day will not be forgotten, not on my watch," said Gerber. But as of May 4, 2010, the future of the Pacific War Museum is cloudy. That day marks the sudden death of John Gerber, dedicated Marine.

Felix P. Camacho, Guam's governor, noted, "John was a true American hero, who proudly served his country as a U.S. Marine and was instrumental in preserving our island's

"John was a true American hero who proudly served his country as a U.S. Marine and was instrumental in preserving our island's World War II history at the Pacific War Museum.

–Felix P. Camacho

Guam's governor

World War II history at the Pacific War Museum. ... John was a proud Marine, who took it upon himself to extend our island's gratitude and hospitality over the years, feeding thousands upon thousands of soldiers at gatherings he hosted at his home in Chalan Pago and was responsible for the renaming of Marine Corps Drive, to recognize the valiant fight of his fellow Marines during World War II."

In his eulogy of John Gerber, Colonel Robert D. Loynd, USMC Liaison to the Territory of Guam, said that upon arriving on Guam for his current tour, one of the first people he met was John Gerber. He noted, "I was meeting a man of tremendous intellect, as I learned more in the first five minutes about Guam's crosscultural history and conflicts than my jetlagged brain could absorb."

Loynd also said that he had been asked to write a letter of recommendation supporting the nomination of John Gerber's Pacific War Museum for the Marine Corps Heritage Foundation's prestigious Colonel John

Above: This tracked landing vehicle was used during the recapture of Guam from the Japanese and is just one of the items John Gerber added to his museum.

Below: Gerber's use of discarded Jetways for indoor exhibits was an economy move that paid off, as visitors enjoy the closeness of the exhibits.

H. Magruder III Award. The award recognizes small museums dedicated to the heritage of the Corps and those who create and operate them.

Loynd quoted his letter of recommendation: "Over the course of the past two decades, no person has done more to honor the history and reputation of the United States Marine Corps on Guam than John Gerber. His Pacific War Museum remains a sole outpost of Marine Corps heritage in the vast mid-Pacific. Visited by Commandants, generals, congressmen, Marines, history enthusiasts, tourists, children and citizens of various nations alike, John's museum both inspires and brings contemplative reflection."

Now, John Gerber's family is intent on ensuring the museum's success. Ryan Gerber, John's son, affirmed that "we are now resolved with the daunting task of keeping the dream alive." John Gerber could ask no more.

Author's note: People recall where they were on momentous days, like "Sept. 11, 2001." On May 4, 2010, sitting in a hotel lobby in Istanbul, I was thunderstruck when Colonel Raymond F. "Frenchy" L'Heureux told me of John Gerber's sudden heart attack and death. A fortnight prior, at the request of Lieutenant General Keith Stalder, I had journeyed to Guam to write a story that would be the genesis of a nomination for the coveted Magruder museum recognition from the Marine Corps Heritage Foundation. In five days, I became John Gerber's friend for life. I will never forget John, never.

Si Yu'us ma'ase' (thank you) to LtGen Keith Stalder, Colonel Bob Loynd, Thelma Zenaida Hechanova, Ramona Robertson, Governor Felix Camacho and Mrs. Mela Gerber who kept us all grounded . . . and once again, mahalo, Ernie Pyle, also not forgotten.

Editor's note: Patrick "P.T." Brent, a frequent Leatherneck contributor, is proud to have been an infantry Marine who served in 2/24. He also was a UPI military correspondent, embedded in Afghanistan, Iraq and Africa.

The Marines have landed
and have the situation well in hand.

Richard Harding Davis

The Song of the Marines

Over the sea, let's go men!

We're shovin' right off, we're shovin' right off again

Nobody knows where or when

We're shovin' right off, we're shovin' right off again

It may be Shanghai, farewell and goodbye

Sally and Sue, don't be blue

We'll just be gone for years and years and then

We're shovin' right off for home, shovin' right off for home

Shovin' right off for home again

Over the sea, lets go men.

We're shovin' right off, we're shovin' right off again

Nobody knows where or when

We're sailin' away, we're sailin' away again.

From the halls of Moctezuma, To the shores of Tripoli

We will fight a raging battle-front

From Sea to Shining Sea

*Here's to America's ship
and America's women.
May they both always be well manned.*

Sterling Harden

author, actor, Taipan and U.S. Marine – World War II

10 November 1969

EPILOGUE

FORT APACHE, AFGHANISTAN

P.T. Brent

15 August 2012

In the past few days, our Corps lost six Marines in Afghanistan, yet there was scant news coverage; what is the matter with us?

Any future defense secretary who advises the President to again send a big American land army into Asia or into the Middle East or Africa should have his head examined.

Secretary of Defense Robert Gates (candid remark before leaving office in July 2011)

Our troops need to come home.

There is one tried and tested solution.

American bravery and sacrifice are stunted by a plan, which was flawed from the beginning and will never work. Afghanistan is a corrupt pseudo democracy that continues to rob us of our precious lives and resources. Billions are squandered for the enrichment of a few. Less than 10 percent of the territory is under effective control. The local police and army are ineffective, untrustworthy and will not stay the course of reform. Sanctuary in Pakistan makes pursuit sublime. Post 10 years of U.S. occupation, 95 percent of the world's opium crop still flourishes. Ten frustrating years and over 300 billion American dollars have been consumed: two million veterans, 300,000 stress cases and rehabilitation–all well earned and deserved, but it will us cost billions.

It is time to curtail the imprudence of this unconvincing "Americanization" of the world. It is, however, not the time to cease destroying terrorists' cells that threaten our country with another 9/11.

Is there anyone who believes we can "Americanize" a country the size of Texas whose customs have had little change since the time of Christ? Is there a rationale to our taxpayers funding of this giant "military/industrial" complex?

We Americans aka "infidels" have freed Afghanistan–and have attempted to create a little Indiana in a culture that wants none of it. One Arab general and an ally once pointed out we can never be brothers. Christians will always be infidels to them. Human rights— that is a concept that will never be embraced in their culture.

America's longest war has linked the United States to the same failed efforts of numerous other failed conquerors and Afghan invaders going back to the time before Christ. In the 1800s, the British failed. Russia failed in the 1900s, once again using a large land force to invade—and ultimately to serve the people of a country who are flummoxed by our presence. It's mind boggling that we are doing this in Afghanistan to the tune of two billion dollars a month with no end in sight. The loss of American lives: priceless.

Solution: Fort Apache

Imagine a string of bases, which are well protected, and in viable range of terrorist activities. Human intelligence and/or drones offer electronic surveillance alerts directing our forces to the enemy. The effectiveness of drones—in terms of both economics and risk management with pilots' lives—is becoming widely acclaimed.

The answer echoes back to the 1800s and the days of the U.S. Cavalry. The soldiers had to protect our country's interests and cover vast land masses with few resources. This will sound familiar to our many Afghan veterans; it was the Wild West. We established a network of forts and intelligence scouts that offered protection at reasonable cost in lives and resources—hopefully, with better oversight and control than we had in the 1800s. Today forts are more sophisticated and unmanned aircraft and state-of-the-art electronics enhance the scout's "Intel." Some are far away and others are on Navy ships at sea.

The French Foreign Legion has practiced the same tactics that our

U.S. Cavalry did in 1870. The cost in human life, as well as the economics, dictate practical imperatives. In Djibouti, Africa, where I went on patrols as a journalist with Marines, this type of outpost may afford the framework of a practical solution. In this forlorn section of the Horn of Africa, the Legionnaries had established Camp Lemoine—now garrisoned by United States Marines and U.S. Army soldiers. When intelligence, whether it is human or electronic, reveals a terrorist training camp, the Marines or Special Forces destroy it. This will deny the enemy command and control centers as well as training bases in areas where they exploit destitute populations. Not much different than the troops back in 1870—just fewer horses, better weaponry and no bugles.

The U.S. Cavalry in 1870 attacked rebellious tribes. The Wild West was far too vast and costly to civilize and govern. After destroying the enemy, our troops could regroup and take shelter within their forts. Compare this to our current situation in which the economics are minuscule compared to the loss of precious life. Dollars are expended at the rate of 2.8 million per hour in Afghanistan.

The majority of our troops need to come home. Virtuous as it may sound, "Americanization" of the world will not work. The pragmatic mission is to fight terrorism overseas before it hits the United States.

Again, our troops need to come home.

Author's Note: This has been the haunting issue since one Easter weekend in OIF where mortuary affairs had a pallet of 32 transfer cases in stock; three days later, only four were remaining. Marines from Ramadi were on a final journey home. Last month, I attended a funeral in Chicago of another Marine KIA from Afghanistan.

U.S. SPENDING ON IRAQ AND AFGHANISTAN BY MONTH, WEEK, DAY, HOUR, MINUTE, & SECOND
(based on adjusted DOD FY 2007 obligations)
Updated February 25, 2008

	Iraq	Afghanistan	Total
Per Month	$10.3 billion	$2 billion	$12.3 billion
Per Week	$2.4 billion	$469 million	$2.9 billion
Per Day	$343 million	$67 million	$410 million
Per Hour	$14 million	$2.8 million	$17 million
Per Minute	$238,425	$46,296	$284,722
Per Second	$3,973	$771	$4,745

SOURCE: Data from Amy Belasco, "The Cost of Iraq, Afghanistan, and Other Global War on Terror Operations Since 9/11," Congressional Research Service (updated February 8, 2008). Totals may not add due to rounding.

www.TheAmercianGeisha.com

AFTERMATH

Well, what's next post exposing my indiscretions to the world? Perhaps now is the best time to go on to the next outrageous book, which is entitled: "The American Geisha."

No doubt, this effort will make the author, a.k.a. Tim Monaghan, the point of derisive abuse from a few western women. Nonetheless, having seen firsthand the mechanical treatment that some western women unfortunately afford the men in their lives, it seems appropriate to offer a modicum of tutoring. *Making the assumption the man is a worthy gentleman, an individual who will enjoy a woman who truly wishes to give him pleasure and understanding.*

This book is for men who are tired of being discouraged and subdued by women and want to change their romantic lives for the better. And, it is a remarkable study for women who have the courage and curiosity to admit that they are willing and want to please their men!

This book is not politically correct nor is it about political correctness. It is about enjoying life. Check the "New York Times" Best Seller List next Christmas . . . hope your lady secured a copy for you.

Visit: www.TheAmercianGeisha.com.

P.T. Brent, Hawaii—10 November 2012

ABOUT THE AUTHOR

From inner city Chicago to Pearl Harbor, Patrick Timothy Brent's story marches to a distinctly different beat. The product of many years of Catholic education, Brent studied to be a Catholic priest for two years before being expelled for breaking most of the rules. One of his guiding philosophies is that it is better to be outrageous than obscure. A born salesman, Brent has always responded to adversity with boldness, ingenuity and integrity. Today, he is a successful entre-preneur, adventurer and avid polo player, but his most cherished titles are that of *Marine* and *father*. A writer by avocation, his most recent stint was as an embedded correspondent for the U.S. Marine Corps in the Operations in Iraq and Afghanistan. These assignments came years after his own active duty service. Upcoming works include a novel, "The American Geisha," and a collaborative work on General John Archer Lejeune (Luh jern).

ABOUT THE ILLUSTRATOR

An artist as long as he can remember, Dan Fowler's interest in art began at a very young age with comic books, cartoons and monster movies. A University of South Carolina Upstate graduate, his career as a freelance multi-media artist has included several diverse jobs ranging from comic strips and children's storybooks to novel cover designs and independent film making. Dan's current project, aside from his continuing freelance jobs, is an independent film he is co-producing called "Bone to the Dog" (www.BonetotheDog.com).

tu ne cede malis sed contra audentior ito

P.T.B. OUT